CW00493728

SERVANTS
of the LORD

SERVANTS
of the LORD

Outdoor Staff at the Great Country Houses

David S. D. Jones

Quiller

Copyright © 2017 David S D Jones

First published in the UK in 2017
by Quiller, an imprint of Quiller Publishing Ltd

British Library Cataloguing-in-Publication Data
A catalogue record for this book is available from the British Library

ISBN 978 1 84689 247 9

Design by Guy Callaby

Black and white photographs and other archive materials are the copyright/property
of the David S. D. Jones Collection unless otherwise stated and credited

Printed in the Czech Republic

Quiller
An imprint of Quiller Publishing Ltd
Wykey House, Wykey, Shrewsbury SY4 1JA
Tel: 01939 261616
Email: info@quillerbooks.com
Website: www.quillerpublishing.com

CONTENTS

Early aerial view of the deer park at Kilverstone Hall, Norfolk. Kilverstone Hall can be seen in the bottom left-hand corner of the photograph, while Kilverstone Church (with round tower) is visible inside the park.

ACKNOWLEDGEMENTS

FIRSTLY, I MUST thank the various friends, relatives, acquaintances and professional colleagues with private service connections who have willingly supplied me with information for this book, have pointed me in the direction of useful sources, or have granted me access to archival material in their custody or possession. In particular, I would like to mention the following: Maureen Brown; Walter Cole; Evelyn Ferrett; Sophia Gallia: Jack Grasse; Eddie Graves MBE; the Fovant History Interest Group; Grant Macfarlane; and Tim Weston.

Special thanks go to Simon North of Strutt & Parker, not only for his assistance with the Land Agent chapter but also for supplying me with information about his father, Commander William North, for many years resident land agent on the Broadlands estate in Hampshire. Thanks also to my friend and colleague Charles Nodder, political adviser to the National Gamekeepers' Organisation, for reading through and correcting the chapters pertaining to the Hunt Establishment and the Game Department.

For evocative memories and recollections of life in outdoor private service in times past, I owe a debt of gratitude to the various elderly country folk whom I have interviewed over the past fifty-five years or so, some of whom were born during the final decades of Queen Victoria's reign. In particular, I must mention: the late Don Ford; June Grass; the late Kate Grass; the late Stella Grass, the late Delmè Jones, the late Tom Jones; the late George Leaning; the late Captain John Rapley; and Barbara Whittle.

Last but not least, I would like to thank Bill Barton, Maureen Brown, Graham Bushell, Christine Hallam, Lord Margadale of Islay, Barbara Whittle, the Lockinge Trust Estate and the Pairc Historical Society for willingly supplying photographs and illustrations for use in this book.

Whilst every reasonable effort has been made to contact all copyright owners in whatever context, if I have omitted anyone or made any errors, I can only apologise and request that those affected contact the publishers in order that amends can be made in any subsequent printing of this edition.

David S. D. Jones
Summer 2017

INTRODUCTION

MUCH HAS BEEN written about life in the country house in recent years, both in terms of the wealthy occupants and the below stairs staff who attended to their needs. Little has been recorded, though, about the servants who worked outside the house and were responsible for ensuring the smooth running of the surrounding estate. These servants, although largely overlooked by historians, were, nevertheless, as important as their indoor counterparts. They played a key role in the development and management of the traditional country estate from the time of the Dissolution of the Monasteries in the mid-sixteenth century, when members of the nobility and gentry began to acquire large tracts of land and to build mansions rather than fortified residences. Their influence lasted until the early 1920s, when all but the most affluent of landowners were forced to scale down estate operations due to the combined effects of high taxation and staff shortages.

The golden age of the country estate

The country estate enjoyed a golden age from the late eighteenth century until the outbreak of World War One in 1914. Every estate, however large or small, whether owned by a wealthy nobleman or a minor landed gentleman, was operated as a self-supporting unit during this period and required a large staff of men to undertake the multitudinous range of tasks that needed to be carried out on a daily basis. Skilled gardeners were employed to care for the gardens and pleasure grounds, which were used for leisure purposes and also provided fresh vegetables, fruit and flowers for the household. Specialist farm workers and general agricultural labourers were retained to run the home farm, which supplied fresh meat and dairy products. Grooms, coachmen and other stable servants were kept to look after the horses and to drive the various horse-drawn vehicles used to transport the owner and his family. Gamekeepers, hunt servants, river keepers and others were employed to provide hunting, shooting and fishing facilities for the owner, members of his family and sporting guests. Building tradesmen and labourers were kept to maintain the mansion and its out offices, the tenant farms, the estate workers' houses and other buildings in good condition, and to carry out alterations or 'new builds' as and when required. Foresters were needed to produce home-grown timber for construction work, fencing and garden use. Itinerant workers were hired regularly, too, to undertake a variety of jobs ranging from hedge laying and drystone walling to mole catching, pig killing and cider making! Last but not least, a resident land agent was employed to manage the

Opposite: The staff at Odiham Priory, a minor Hampshire country house, c1870. The outdoor servants are standing in the back row, wearing hats. George Sclater Booth, MP (later 1st Lord Basing), the owner of the property, was interested in the arts rather than sport so did not require a large complement of men to look after his small estate.

Right: Early aerial view of part of the Kilverstone estate, Norfolk, 1913. Kilverstone Hall appears on the extreme left below the church (with round tower). The home farm, the estate yard and workshops, and the walled gardens can be seen in the foreground.

Below: Chauffeur posing casually beside his employer's car in front of the garage at a Hampshire country house c1910. The garage has been converted either from a coach house or part of a stable and has a staff flat above.

entire estate operation on behalf of the owner and to act as his business representative when dealing with staff, tenants and others on day-to-day matters.

A resident clergyman, a fire brigade, a menagerie keeper, a hermit …

Most estates employed a resident Church of England clergyman to act as vicar or chaplain of the owner's private chapel or church, situated either in the mansion house or the grounds. Many retained a private fire brigade of some description, comprising entirely of staff members, who were paid a small monthly bonus in addition to their wages for attending weekly drill sessions. Some large properties numbered a hermit, a menagerie keeper, an agister, a golf professional, a team of railway men (to operate a private railway) or other specialist employees among the outdoor servants. From the late Victorian period onwards the advent of new technology in the form of the motor car and the electric lighting plant necessitated the recruitment of a chauffeur, and an electrician to augment the existing staff at all but the poorest of establishments. Prior to the passage of the Education Act in 1870, which paved the way for free state education, a surprising number of enlightened landowners also kept a school teacher on the staff to run an 'estate school' for the benefit of the children of servants and tenants.

Superior working conditions and job security

Outdoor servants on a country estate, like their below stairs colleagues who worked in the mansion, were generally much better off than those employed by tenant farmers and small village businesses or as unskilled labourers in factories in towns and cities. Notwithstanding the relatively low wages paid by many landowners, staff had job security provided that they performed their duties to a satisfactory standard, and benefited from a range of perquisites including free clothing, fuel, tips, surplus game, Christmas boxes and, last but not least, accommodation. Some employers also operated a sick pay scheme and paid a retainer to the local doctor in order that he could provide medical treatment to anyone who was ill.

Employees housed according to status

Employees were housed according to their status within the estate hierarchy. The land agent and the clergymen, both of whom were often related to the landowner, usually resided in a large detached house or a substantial vicarage set in its own grounds and retained their own small staff of servants. The head gamekeeper, the head gardener, the clerk of works and other departmental heads invariably lived in a four- or five-bed- roomed detached house and, if lucky, might have their own maid servant,

Gardener on a country estate c1900. His emoluments invariably included free housing and fuel, a supply of fresh vegetables and various other perquisites.

11

while the farm bailiff lived in the home farmhouse and the head coachman had his quarters in an apartment above the stables. Married staff lower down the scale either lived in a two- or three bed-roomed cottage in the estate village, a farm worker's or a gamekeeper's cottage set amidst the woods or fields, a lodge at the entrance to one of the driveways or in a flat above the out offices adjacent to the mansion. Single men were generally accommodated in dormitories or small bedrooms in the mansion out offices, lived in the gardeners' or the gamekeepers' bothy (hostel), lodged with a senior member of staff in their own particular department or, exceptionally, had a room in the servants' quarters in the mansion, itself.

The head gamekeeper's house on the Bix estate near Henley-on-Thames, Oxfordshire, 1920. Detached and standing in its own grounds, the property reflects the status of the occupant within the staff hierarchy.

A 'closed world'

Life for the outdoor servant in the 'closed world' of the country estate, although not always idyllic, was well ordered and generally not too strenuous as the more traditional landowners preferred a job to be well done rather than rushed. Families often worked on the same property for several generations, carrying out the same trade on a father-to-son basis. If working conditions were good, men would spend a lifetime in a relatively minor position on an estate rather than move away to obtain promotion and a higher wage. Long-serving staff were usually provided with a cottage for life, were either given less strenuous work in old age or were expected to help out at busy times only, and, if fortunate, they might receive a small pension or annuity from their

employer. In contrast, anyone who continuously moved from one position to another for whatever reason could expect to end his days either living with a relative or in the local workhouse prior to the introduction of the state pension in 1909.

Entrance lodge on a Suffolk estate c1890. Home to an under-keeper – whose wife would have been responsible for opening and closing the gates – the building was designed to be functional as well as aesthetically pleasing.

Mr and Mrs Hartles, pensioners on the Bentley estate in Worcestershire, outside their cottage 1912. Mr Hartles undertook light work in the timber yard from time to time, for which he was paid independently of his pension.

The 1909 People's Budget

Presented to Parliament by the Liberal Chancellor of the Exchequer, David Lloyd George, and his young ally, Winston Churchill, President of the Board of Trade, in 1909 and passed in 1910, the People's Budget enabled the government to raise money to pay for new social welfare schemes by levying additional taxes on land and high incomes. This affected all country estate owners, particularly those of moderate means, some of whom were obliged to reduce staff numbers in order to meet their tax obligations. Indeed, one head gamekeeper employed on a Scottish estate who was made redundant because of the Budget wrote the following letter to the editor of *The Gamekeeper* magazine in December 1909:

Sir,

THE BUDGET: MORE UNEMPLOYMENT
I suppose you do not know of a head keepers situation going at the end of the season. I have lived here five years with Mr A. who will be pleased to give me five years excellent character. He is giving up rearing and reducing the establishment all round, keepers, gardeners and foresters, all through the Budget. He says that he will have to sell half of the estate to live and I am afraid there will be a great many more like him round this country. I can show twenty three years good character as head keeper both in England and Scotland, so if you know, or hear of a place going you might kindly let me know. I hope there will not be any brother keepers who vote Liberal, if they do, they ought to give up the trade.

The effects of World War One

Sadly, the declaration of World War One sounded the death knell for the traditional country estate. In the region of 400,000 male servants, both outdoor and indoor, joined the armed services in order to fight for King and country, many of whom were killed or injured on the battlefield or the high seas, or chose not to return to private service after the conflict had ended. Those too old to go to war worked on farms or in vegetable gardens, became temporary foresters, kept shoots ticking over, controlled vermin and carried out numerous other essential tasks, with the assistance of land girls, German prisoners of war, conscientious objectors and others. Estates fell into neglect due to a lack of manpower, grass land and deer parks were ploughed up for food production purposes, mature woodlands were felled to provide timber for the war effort, pleasure gardens were often abandoned in their entirety, horses were requisitioned for the Army, vast tracts of land were taken over by the government for military usage, while country houses were turned into hospitals and convalescent homes for wounded servicemen.

Change beyond all recognition

The country estate has changed beyond all recognition since the cessation of hostilities in 1918. Properties have been reduced in size for financial reasons, tenant farms and woodlands have been sold off, areas of land have been turned into golf courses, country parks or military training grounds, while country houses have been handed over to organisations such as the National Trust or English Heritage in order to preserve them for future generations, utilised for schools, hotels, nursing homes

Soldiers posing for the camera in front of a prefabricated wooden barracks at one of the numerous temporary Army camps erected on country estates during World War One

or other institutional and commercial purposes, converted into apartments or, in some instances, demolished in their entirety. Modern farm and garden machinery has obviated the need to employ large numbers of outdoor servants, at the same time compensating for staff shortages and ever increasing wage bills.

Didlington Hall, Norfolk, 1912. Purchased by the banker, Colonel Herbert Smith in 1910 from Baroness Amherst, the property served as a family home until World War Two, when it was requisitioned by the Army and used as headquarters for General Miles Dempsey, Commander of the British Second Army during the D-Day landings. In common with many other country houses, the hall suffered from damage and neglect during the military occupation and was subsequently stripped of its fixtures and fittings prior to demolition in the early 1950s.

Business-orientated landowners

Landowners have had to become business orientated over the past century or so in order to survive. Estates have had to change from being private fiefdoms run solely for the benefit of the proprietor and his family – often at a loss – to financially self-supporting entities capable of making a profit. Country houses have been opened to the public as 'stately homes', farms have been taken in hand and are farmed by agricultural contractors rather than estate staff, woodlands are either managed by specialist forestry contractors or leased out, building work is also carried out by contractors on most estates, fishing on rivers and lakes has been made available to members of the public on a fee-paying basis, shoots have been turned into commercial operations specifically to derive an income from paying Guns, while firms of professional land agents now undertake all estate management work on the great majority of properties.

Outdoor servants today

Outdoor servants continue to be employed on country estates today, albeit on a much smaller scale than in the past. Gamekeepers, gardeners, river keepers, hunt servants, grooms and other equestrian staff are still very much in demand, although most now

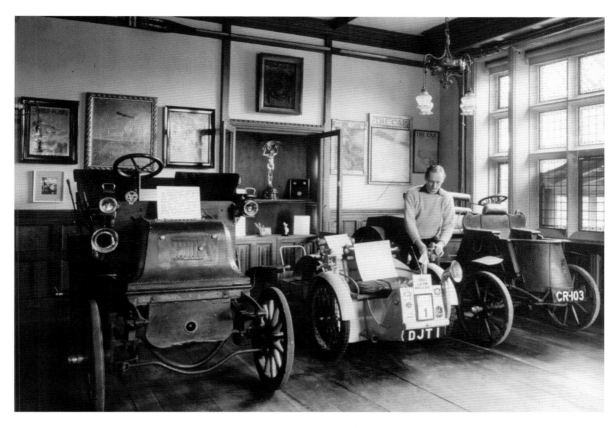

work on a single-handed basis rather than as part of a team. Some landowners also retain other in-house estate workers, many of whom are expected to 'multi-task', as and when required, but this is becoming increasingly less common due to high employment costs and the lack of affordable housing in rural areas.

Edward, Lord Montagu of Beaulieu, one of the most successful of the early stately home pioneers, who transformed Beaulieu in Hampshire from a traditional country estate into a world-class tourist attraction, not only opening Palace House and the Abbey ruins to the public but also establishing the National Motor Museum in 1952. The leading expert on stately homes during the late twentieth century, he became the first president of the Historic Houses Association, served as the chairman of English Heritage and was an active member of the House of Lords. Courtesy of the National Motor Museum, Beaulieu.

Modern day servants of the lord: members of Lord Margadale's property maintenance team carrying out groundwork on the Fonthill estate, Wiltshire, 2017.

The Thornham Estate in 1933

Gamekeeper Harry Grass moved from the Lambton Castle estate in County Durham to take a beat keeper's position at Thornham Hall near Eye in Suffolk in 1933. The estate, owned by the 6th Lord Henniker since 1902, was still being run along late nineteenth century lines, with a full complement of craftsmen capable of undertaking virtually any task allotted to them. Recalling his arrival at Thornham in later life, along with his first impressions of the estate, Harry wrote:

I was met at the railway station by the head keeper who was driving a pony cart. He was dressed somewhat old-fashioned, or at least it seemed so to me, in a semi-frock coat, breeches and box cloth leggings. Very little was said by either of us as we drove the five miles to his house but as we travelled down the narrow country roads I saw thatched cottages with pink cream washed walls and I got the feeling that I had moved back in time by something like 50 years for I had not seen anything quite like it before.

Farm workers with horses on the Thornham estate, 1935.

Harry Grass (on left)
with Thornham head
keeper, Harold Chandler,
1935.

*In the course of the next few days I met the rest of the gamekeepers
and while we had dialect difficulties, and did so for quite some time, we all
spoke 'keepers language', but I was in a completely different world, this was
true country, untouched by anything modern. Where country craftsmen
carried out their duties using methods which if they had ever existed in the
North had vanished long before my time. I saw men making large farm
wagons and tumbrils. Farm methods and cropping were not the same, there
were no heavy shire horses, no hills but completely flat ground. Even the
weather was different. Unless one's memory is at fault the summers were all
warm and dry.*

*The estate was a country factory, everyone in the locality was employed
on it. Men of all professions, foresters, sawyers, carpenters, painters, farm
workers. They even made their own bricks and field drain pipes in moulds.
The estate was self-supporting in every way and was owned and governed
by a truly country gentleman, affectionately called 'the little old man'
whose knowledge of country lore and gun-dogs was of a very high standard
indeed.*

THE LAND AGENT

THE SENIOR OUTDOOR servant on a country estate, the resident land agent not only managed the property on behalf of the owner but also acted as his representative, conducting day-to-day business with staff, tenants and others. His duties were many and varied, ranging from liaising with different heads of departments, hiring and firing employees, letting farms and cottages, supervising the sale of timber and farm produce and overseeing property maintenance and building works, to running the estate office, keeping accounts, paying wages and other estate outgoings, and collecting rents. He was usually provided with a sizeable detached house and a salary commensurate with his status, and was expected to be able to mix with his employer and his guests on an equal footing as and when required. More often than not he was an impoverished relative, friend or former service colleague of a landed proprietor, chosen as much for his skill with rod and gun as for his ability to manage men, transact business and keep estates accounts and other records.

Land stewards or bailiffs

Known originally as land stewards or bailiffs, land agents were first employed during the seventeenth century by wealthy noblemen to collect rents, keep accounts and supervise farming operations on large properties. Such men became increasingly important during the Georgian period as estates were expanded through the enclosure of open fields and common land and developed for agricultural, forestry and sporting purposes. On small estates at this time, it was not uncommon for the land agent to be a tenant farmer, combining farming activities with land stewardship. He might also act as woodward and head gamekeeper.

Some of the more progressive landowners, particularly those with large estates or who owned several properties, started to employ land agents who were experienced in farming, surveying or the law during the first half of the nineteenth century rather than relatives, friends or, in some instances, former butlers, farm bailiffs and other senior servants. Scotsmen were often recruited as agents on 'flagship' estates as they were considered to be more conscientious than their English counterparts and invariably devoted more time to business affairs than to field sports. The 1ˢᵗ Earl

Opposite: John Dow (on left), land agent to the 2ⁿᵈ Earl of Iveagh, on the 23,000 acre Elveden estate in Suffolk with his assistant Mr H.E. 'Ted' Crane, 1952. A Scotsman, Mr Dow was appointed to the post in 1921 and held office for around forty years.

of Leicester, the great agriculturalist, for example, appointed Francis Blaikie as his agent at Holkham Hall in Norfolk; the well-known agricultural improver, Sir James Graham, Bt., employed John Yule, from a Scottish farming background, as agent on the Netherby estate in Cumberland; Sir Robert Peel, Bt., engaged John Matthew, another farmer, as his agent at Drayton Manor in Staffordshire. Scottish land agents usually hired fellow Scotsmen as head foresters, head gamekeepers and farm bailiffs to work beneath them wherever possible.

Samuel and Sarah Adams provide some guidance for a newly employed land agent in *The Complete Servant*, published in 1825:

On his first entering into office, he should make a general survey of all the estates and property entrusted in his care:- he should also form an inventory, and open a set of books on a clear and perspicuous plan, if not already done by his predecessor, taking care to enter in them a correct list of all the books, writings, deeds, schedules, court-rolls, &c. From this survey, whether left by his predecessor, or taken by himself, regular memorandums should be made in a book, of everything necessary to be remarked or executed, of the places where deficiencies are found, or improvements may be made; of buildings and repairs necessary; insurances, dates of leases, rates, nuisances, trespasses, live and dead stock, game, timber, fencing, draining, paths and roads, culture, commons, rivers, and sea coasts, and of every other specific article relative to his trust, which deserves attention, and therefore ought not to be committed to loose papers, or left to memory.

The need for a professional training system for land agents

Land agency work became increasingly complicated as the nineteenth century progressed. Agents on estates with collieries or mineral workings, or which were traversed by canals or railways, not only needed to be land managers but also required a working knowledge of accountancy, the law, surveying and other subjects in order to carry out their duties effectively and in the best interests of their employer. The need for some kind of professional training system for land agents had become apparent, yet little guidance was available other than from professional men, fellow land agents and manuals such as *The Book of the Landed Estate* by Robert Brown, published in 1869.

In 1896 the Royal Commission on the Land of Wales and Monmouthshire set down what it took to be the proper training of a land agent:

We think that such (an) agent should be one who in addition to a sound preliminary, general, and scientific education has received a special theoretical training in agriculture and land surveying, and in the sciences (such as mathematics, chemistry etc.) upon which the practise of these arts depends, as well as practical experience in an estate office and on a farm. To put the matter in another way, we think a young man, intending to become a land agent should, in addition to acquiring the average degree of culture and knowledge of a university man, attend courses of study at an agricultural college or a college giving technical instruction in the practical arts, and then pass some time gaining practical and actual experience in an office or on a farm. In short, we would have him prepare himself professionally in a manner analogous to that in which the physician qualifies himself to practice the art of medicine, or a solicitor that of the law.

The Country Gentlemen's Estate Book 1916. Published annually by the Country Gentlemen's Association Ltd, the book was a standard work of reference for land agents and landowners alike, containing up-to-date information relating to all aspects of estate management.

Impecunious but well-connected land agents

Notwithstanding the need for professionally qualified land agents at this time, especially given the impact of industrialisation and rapidly changing agricultural practices on many country estates during the course of the Victorian period, some major landowners continued to employ impecunious relatives and friends to manage their property until the mid-twentieth century, often with the assistance of a sub-agent (deputy agent), usually a former gamekeeper or farm bailiff of long standing or a senior estate office clerk. The 2nd Duke of Westminster, for example, employed his uncle, the Honourable Cecil Parker, as his land agent for the Eaton estate in Cheshire from 1899 until 1910; the 7th Lord Henniker employed his younger brother, the Honourable John Henniker, as land agent on the Thornham estate in Suffolk from 1932 until 1956; Owen Smith, owner of the Langham estate in Rutland, engaged his niece's husband, the Honourable Charles FitzRoy as his land agent in 1927, a post that he held until he succeeded as 10th Duke of Grafton in 1936 following the death of a cousin.

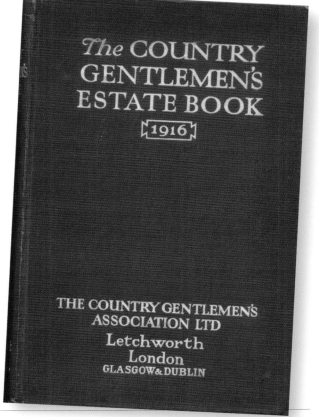

Land agency in the post-World War One era

In the aftermath of World War One, it was not uncommon for landowners with small estates, or those hit by high taxation or death duties, to dispense with a resident land agent and use a local auctioneer or a solicitor to carry out land agency duties on a part-time basis or to undertake the work themselves with the aid of a secretary. Several sons of landed proprietors even trained as land agents during the 1920s and '30s. Henry Thynne, Viscount Weymouth and later 6th Marquess of Bath, for instance, became a pupil land agent at Lockinge Park in Oxfordshire in 1927 in order that he could run the Longleat estate in Wiltshire himself upon his succession to the property, while Viscount Mandeville, eldest son of the 9th Duke of Manchester, actually served as agent on the family estate at Kimbolton Castle in Huntingdonshire from 1930 until 1939. Some impoverished landowners, however, who saw it as something of a status symbol to retain a resident land agent, recruited retired Army officers for the role, providing them with a 'grace and favour' house and a small salary to augment their pension along with sporting facilities in return for managing their property in a somewhat amateur manner. These men, who were generally more interested in the country way of life than in the job itself, were not infrequently dubbed as 'Major disaster', 'General catastrophe' or similar by staff and tenants alike!

Resident land agents continued to be employed on many large and medium-sized estates until the 1950s and '60s. Thereafter, owners of such properties started to engage firms of professional land agents such as Cluttons, Strutt & Parker or Saville's to act as agents on their behalf, recognising they were better suited than an in-house land agent when dealing with the multitude of rules and regulations relating to agriculture, land ownership and taxation that had been imposed by successive post-war governments. The great majority continued to retain an estate office, though, employing a small secretarial staff to handle day-to-day estate business. Today, the land agent, resident or otherwise, is something of a rarity, even on very large country estates.

The sub-agent

Employed to assist the land agent on a large estate, the sub-agent dealt with 'run of the mill' enquiries and complaints from staff and tenants, and deputised for him in his absence. He was either a farm bailiff, a gamekeeper or other outdoor servant of long standing who had been promoted to the position because of his intimate knowledge of the workings of an estate and his ability to get on with the tenantry, or a newly trained agent gaining land management experience before applying for a situation of his own. Some sub-agents were based on a detached portion of an estate, which they managed on a day-to-day basis on behalf of the land agent.

The estate office

Found on country estates both large and small from the Victorian period onwards, the estate office provided clerical support for the land agent and the various heads of departments. Supervised by the head clerk, who worked in close collaboration with the agent, the staff on a large property might include a couple of general clerks who dealt with correspondence and similar matters, a pay clerk, a book keeper of some description, a telegraph and telephone operator, and a private secretary who looked after the landowner's personal clerical affairs. Estate office staff were generally male rather than female!

Thomas Arch (1832–1898), sub-agent to the Powell family on the Strata Florida Abbey estate in Cardiganshire from 1873 until 1898. A native of Northamptonshire, he had moved to Cardiganshire in 1854 to become gamekeeper on the Powell's principal estate at Nanteos near Aberystwyth.

Commander William North – land agent

Commander William North served as land agent on the Broadlands estate in Hampshire from the mid-1920s until his retirement in 1960. Grandson of the 11th Lord North, he was a land agent of the 'old school', much respected by staff and tenants alike. An enthusiastic sportsman, he was not only a good shot but also regularly rode to hounds with the Hursley Hunt, and, along with the well-known equestrian artist, Lionel Edwards, was a member of the committee that kept the hunt running during World War Two. He also served as Honorary Secretary of the hunt for many years.

Born in 1898, the commander was educated at the Royal Naval Colleges at Osborne and Dartmouth and served at sea in the Navy throughout World War One. Shortly after the cessation of hostilities in 1918, he went to Trinity Hall at Cambridge to study land management prior to becoming a pupil land agent with a firm of land agents at Brockenhurst in the New Forest. Having gained both academic and practical experience in land agency, he secured a position as an assistant agent with the 4th Duke of Wellington on the 10,000 acre Stratfield Saye estate in Hampshire. He subsequently worked as an assistant agent for the 3rd Viscount Portman at Bryanston near Blandford in Dorset.

In the mid-1920s, Colonel Wilfred Ashley, M.P., later Lord Mount Temple of

continued overleaf

Lee, appointed the commander as his resident land agent on the 6,000 acre Broadlands estate at Romsey in Hampshire, which boasted a 4-mile stretch of the river Test. In addition to managing the property, which included four dairy farms, a piggery, a forestry department and associated sawmill, a productive salmon and trout fishery, and a medium-sized country house shoot looked after by four gamekeepers, he was also responsible for letting and maintaining the tenant farms and cottages, supervising the outdoor staff and farming the 500 acre home farm. He was expected to represent his employer at funerals and other functions, too.

The commander regularly worked from 5 a.m. until after dark. He spent much of his time in the estate office carrying out administrative duties, and would ride around the estate on a hunter early in the morning several times a week inspecting livestock, crops, fences, gates and buildings. Throughout World War Two he served with Combined Operations at a Navy shore station near Southampton during the mornings and managed the Broadlands estate in the afternoons.

Following the death of Lord Mount Temple of Lee in July 1939, the Broadlands estate passed to his son-in-law and daughter, Lord and Lady Louis Mountbatten (later Earl and Countess Mountbatten of Burma). The commander stayed on as land agent at their request until his retirement from ill health in 1960. During his service with the Mountbattens he was not only responsible for making the arrangements for the Royal honeymoon

Commander William North, 1949. *Courtesy of B. Whittle*

at Broadlands after the wedding of Lord Mountbatten's nephew, Lt Philip Mountbatten (now Prince Philip, Duke of Edinburgh) to Princess Elizabeth (now HM the Queen) in 1947, but also for organising tours round the home farm whenever members of the Royal family stayed on the estate – the buildings were freshly painted for these occasions and enormous wicker baskets full of fresh flowers were placed around the farmyard and stables!

Commander North passed away in 1977 aged seventy-nine, one of the last of the traditional breed of land agents. Earl Mountbatten of Burma, who gave the eulogy at his funeral, told the congregation: '"Bill" North ran the whole 6,000 acres of Broadlands immaculately, without the modern aid of computers. He was a true friend.'

Simon North, the commander's eldest son, recalls: 'My father led the idyllic life of an old-fashioned resident land agent, and was very fond both of the Mountbattens and the estate. He also kept his hunters in the stableyard at Broadlands in order to hunt whenever possible with the Hursley Foxhounds.'

2

THE GAME DEPARTMENT

PRESIDED OVER BY the head gamekeeper, the most important outdoor servant on many country estates in times past, the game department is responsible for rearing game birds for shooting purposes, controlling vermin, carrying out poaching prevention and security duties and organising shoots for a landowner and his guests. In contrast to other estate 'trades', many of which have now become obsolete or have changed beyond all recognition, the gamekeeper has survived into the twenty-first century and gamekeeping continues to be carried out today, not only on sporting properties with private shooting facilities but also on commercial shoots that are operated as profit-making businesses.

Shooting party on a country estate c1930. In times past, a landowner relied upon his head gamekeeper to organise these occasions with little or no input from himself other than inviting guests.

The gamekeeper

The term generally applied by members of the public to anyone actively engaged in gamekeeping, irrespective of their position, the gamekeeper is a talented and multi-skilled individual who gives selflessly of his time, working long hours in all weathers to provide and protect his employer's game birds and ground game. His principal duties involve rearing, releasing and feeding game birds on low ground shoots; controlling avian and ground vermin humanely and legally; prevention of poaching; organising shooting days; and recruiting beaters, pickers-up and, in some cases, loaders. On a large estate, he will be in charge of the gun room and might be expected to breed and train gun dogs. He must be something of a diplomat, too, capable of communicating effectively and respectfully with sportsmen, farmers and other country folk, and members of the general public such as ramblers or dog walkers who traverse his preserves on footpaths or bridleways.

Gamekeeper and his wife on a Northumberland estate, 1900. Seen by many simply as a man with a dog and a gun who does little else than walk around the countryside dressed in tweeds, he is in fact an extremely hard-working and multi-talented individual.

A familiar figure in the countryside

Since the late seventeenth century, the gamekeeper has been a familiar figure in the countryside. Initially employed to protect game birds from the predations of poachers, to maintain stocks of wild partridges and other quarry birds by trapping and snaring vermin and to attend gentleman on the shooting field when game shooting was in its infancy, he had become a skilled craftsman by the late Georgian period and had started to preserve pheasants and partridges for sporting purposes through nest

management or by collecting and artificially incubating their eggs using broody hens. Until the early nineteenth century, however, gamekeepers remained fairly thin on the ground, with few landowners employing more than one or two keepers. The Game Act of 1831 removed the property qualification for killing game, enabling any purchaser of a Game Certificate to go out in pursuit of game on a farm or estate provided that he had the owner's permission to do so. However, as late as 1837, when shooting was really starting to become popular in the wake of the Act, official statistics issued by the government estimate that the nation's gamekeeping force consisted only of around 8,000 men.

From the 1840s onwards, gamekeeping changed dramatically. The European practice of 'battue' or driven game shooting, popularised by Prince Albert, the Prince Consort, followed by the introduction of the breech-loading shotgun, which enabled a sportsman to kill a large number of game birds within a short space of time, suddenly created a demand for large stocks of pheasants and partridges and for gamekeepers who could produce and preserve them.

Large teams of gamekeepers

Country landowners now started to recruit large teams of gamekeepers to artificially rear pheasants using broody hens, to preserve partridges through nest management and to bolster hare stocks by putting down imported live hares, in order that big bags of game could be shot on their property. Head gamekeepers were appointed to take charge of game preservation on sporting estates, to allocate work to beat keepers who looked after a 'beat' or section of an estate, to train young men as additional keepers and to liaise with other estate staff. Unlike other outdoor servants, who dealt with their master via a land agent, the head keeper usually had direct access to him!

Throughout the late Victorian and Edwardian periods, a head gamekeeper on a large sporting property might be in charge of a staff of fifteen or more men, including beat keepers, under-keepers, woodmen, trappers, and, sometimes, a deer park keeper. Not only was he responsible for rearing tens of thousands of pheasants annually but he was empowered to dictate the cropping patterns on the tenant farms, ensuring that they were in the best interests of game preservation, and was often in charge of forestry activities such as covert planting and ride widening. If head keeper on a grouse moor, he would invariably control the shepherds and regulate sheep stocks in order that grouse were given priority over sheep.

The gamekeeping staff at Rendlesham Hall, Suffolk, c1890.

The Edwardian era

Gamekeeping, as a profession, reached its peak during the Edwardian era when driven game shooting dominated the fieldsports scene, with landowners competing with each other to provide their guests with daily bags of more than 1,000 pheasants. During this period the number of gamekeepers employed on British estates increased from 17,000 men in 1900 to 23,000 in 1911. Shooting on a grand scale continued unabated until the outbreak of World War One, when sporting operations were scaled down on country estates after keepers and other staff were recruited into the armed services to fight for their country.

Unfortunately, some of the gamekeepers who had survived the war were made redundant during the early 1920s as landowners started to cut back on shoot expenditure due to the effects of high taxation. It was not uncommon during the inter-war years for a gamekeeper on a small estate to combine his duties with farm or forestry work if a shoot was reduced in size or converted from driven to walked-up. By 1939, the number of gamekeepers employed in Great Britain had dropped to an estimated 10,000 men.

World War Two and beyond

Shooting and gamekeeping suffered a further setback during World War Two after sporting estates were banned from rearing game birds and were ordered to cull stocks of pheasants and partridges to provide food for the war effort. Some keepers joined the armed forces for the duration while others served in the Home Guard – where their knowledge of firearms and fieldcraft skills stood them in good stead – or became full-time pest control officers at factories or munitions depots.

Berkshire gamekeeper, Ronald Bushell (on left with his pointer, Trixie, at a field trials) served as a private soldier in the Parachute Regiment during World War Two. He was taken prisoner in the aftermath of the Battle of Arnhem in 1944 and was subsequently posted to a hut-making plant in Germany where he was treated well by his captors. *Courtesy of Graham Bushell*

Following the cessation of hostilities in 1945, government-imposed game bird rearing restrictions, which remained in force until the mid-1950s, made it difficult for all but the wealthiest of landowners to rebuild a shoot. Indeed, other than on very large estates, where a team of gamekeepers continued to be employed, most keepers now worked on a single-handed basis, often carrying out various other duties ranging from gardening to acting as part-time chauffeur!

Since the 1960s, however, the interest in shooting has increased dramatically, fuelled by the growing demand for syndicate shooting and commercially let days, with the result that in the region of 3,000 men (and around 100 women) continue to be employed as full-time gamekeepers in Great Britain at the present time. In addition, the various bodies that represent the shooting industry estimate that a similar number of men are currently involved in gamekeeping on a part-time basis, either assisting professional keepers during their spare time or through participation in small self-keepering shoots.

The gamekeeper today

The gamekeeper of today can best be described as a 'countryside manager'. Unlike his predecessors who were trained 'on the job' in the game department of a country estate, he is likely to have spent some time learning his trade at a countryside college and will be fully conversant with game meat hygiene procedures, firearms regulations, wildlife and countryside legislation and public access matters in order that he can carry out his duties effectively. Indeed, for the past four decades or so education has played an important part in gamekeeper training and must continue to do so in order that the profession of gamekeeping can survive the vicissitudes of the twenty-first century!

Andrew Hyslop, head gamekeeper to the 12th Lord Barnard at Raby Castle, Co. Durham, 2017. *Courtesy of Lindsay Waddell*

The gamekeeping hierarchy

Some large sporting properties or commercial shoots continue to maintain a small game department, with a head gamekeeper, two or three under-keepers and a trainee. Most modern day estates and shoots, however, only employ one gamekeeper who works on a single-handed basis, assisted during busy periods by farm staff, friends or volunteers interested in taking up gamekeeping. In times past, a strict hierarchy existed within the gamekeeping profession, starting with the head keeper at the top and finishing with the dog boy at the bottom, not to mention the numerous part-time staff engaged to assist with shoot day and bird rearing duties ranging from beaters and loaders to nightmen and pheasant tenters.

The head gamekeeper

The man in charge of the game department on a large country estate, the head gamekeeper controls all aspects of game and shoot management. He is usually directly responsible to the landowner rather than the land agent and is sometimes involved in marketing and selling shoot days if a shoot is operated along commercial or semi-commercial lines. In addition to supervising a team of under-gamekeepers, he might also look after a fishery or a deer park.

The second keeper

Something of a rarity today, the second keeper acts as deputy head keeper or foreman over the game department on a large sporting estate. In times past, where an estate was fragmented, a landowner might employ several second keepers under the control of a senior estate official. For example, in the 1930s, the 2nd Duke of Westminster employed two foreman gamekeepers, George Grass and Fred Milton, on his Eaton estate in Cheshire, who reported to Sandy Myles, the head forester.

Jim Grass (on left), head gamekeeper to the 10th Earl Fitzwilliam at Wentworth Woodhouse, Yorkshire, c1970.

The beat keeper

A senior gamekeeper manages a section of an estate known as a 'beat'. Usually based in a cottage on his 'beat', he is responsible for game bird preservation, eradication of vermin and poaching prevention within the area of his jurisdiction. Prior to the outbreak of World War One, it was not unusual for a beat keeper to have his own small team of under-keepers to assist him.

The under-keeper

Upon completion of five or six years' service on a large estate a trainee gamekeeper would traditionally be promoted to under-keeper or junior under-keeper and work beneath a beat keeper, who might control three or four men covering an area of perhaps 2,000 acres. Smaller establishments rarely employed under-keepers, grading every assistant keeper as a beat keeper. On some estates an under-keeper was expected to lodge with the beat keeper to whom he was assigned. In recent years the term 'under-keeper' has been used to describe any keeper below the rank of head gamekeeper.

Group of under-keepers with pheasant rearing coops at Hintlesham Hall, Suffolk, 1906.

Charles Grass, a trainee keeper on the Rendlesham Hall estate in Suffolk c1875.

The trainee keeper

Some of the more progressive late nineteenth century landowners with 'flagship' country house shoots began to recruit school leavers directly as trainee or junior keepers rather than as dog boys. Occasionally, a youth would serve a five- or a seven-year indentured apprenticeship as a gamekeeper, but this was not common practice. Starting salaries varied tremendously from estate to estate. For example, in 1884, the 3rd Earl Manvers employed three junior keepers at Thoresby park in Nottinghamshire, paying them 2/6d (12½p) a day each. Yet as late as 1924, the 3rd Earl of Durham was content to pay his trainee keepers at Lambton Castle in Co. Durham a paltry 6/- (30p) a week.

Prior to the outbreak of World War Two, it was customary for the junior keepers to live in the gamekeepers' bothy on an estate, along with the unmarried under-keepers. On the more prestigious estates, this establishment was presided over by a male housekeeper who ensured that meals were provided and that washing was regularly sent to the estate laundry. On smaller estates, however, the men were expected to cook for themselves using provisions supplied from the 'big house'.

The trainee keeper of today will usually begin his career by attending a residential gamekeeping course at one of a number of specialist countryside colleges, gaining practical experience as well as studying for a relevant vocational qualification. Successful completion of a training course does not automatically guarantee that a student will find a job though, as gamekeeping jobs are now few and far between and are highly sought after.

The dog boy

Until the early years of the twentieth century, it was usual for a school leaver entering the gamekeeping profession to spend a year or so as a dog boy, learning how to manage gun dogs, before being assigned to a beat keeper to begin his training as a gamekeeper. In addition to feeding and exercising dogs and cleaning out kennels, he was often expected to run errands and carry out odd jobs for the head gamekeeper.

The kennelman

Employed to look after the gun and security dogs on an estate, the kennelman might also act as an in-house gun dog trainer and breeder. Now an obsolete rank in the gamekeeping hierarchy, apart from on a few very large sporting properties, he reports directly to the head gamekeeper or to the landowner, himself.

David Eaton, kennelman and under-keeper to the 6th Duke of Portland at Welbeck Abbey, Nottinghamshire with the estate gun dogs 1936.

The single-handed keeper

A gamekeeper with sole responsibility for preserving game and running a shoot on an estate or a farm. This is a relatively new position in the gamekeeping profession, having been introduced during the mid-twentieth century due to the need for economy in estate management.

Cyril Veall (centre), single-handed keeper and forester to Major Richard Wellesley on the Buckland estate in Oxfordshire from 1963 until his death in 1980. *Courtesy of the Veall family*

The warrener

The occupation of warrener dates back to the Middle Ages when the Normans first introduced the rabbit into Great Britain. In East Anglia and other parts of the country where rabbits were artificially reared for food purposes in times past, landowners employed warreners to construct and maintain the mounds or warrens that housed the rabbits, to feed and cull the resident rabbit population, as well as to carry out vermin control and poaching prevention duties. During the nineteenth century, it became the practice for the warrening team on an estate to be placed under the control of the head gamekeeper in order to avoid a conflict of interests between rabbit production and shooting. At Audley End, in Essex, at this time, the 3rd Lord Braybrooke employed a total of three warreners (who were paid £11-7/-6d (£11.37½) per quarter), each of whom was assigned to one particular beat keeper, who directed his work. Warreners continued to be employed on a number of East Anglian estates until the mid-twentieth century but are rarely found today.

The trapper

During the late Victorian and the Edwardian periods, when the sport of game shooting was in its heyday, many large country estates employed two or three full-time trappers under the direction of the head gamekeeper in order that the gamekeepers could devote their time solely to game bird rearing and preservation. Sometimes these men were shared between the game department and the head gardener, who used them to trap moles and other vermin that could damage lawns and flower beds. A trapper was usually paid slightly more than a farm labourer but a little less than a keeper. For example, in 1907, Ernest Turrington, trapper to Edward Miller-Mundy at Thetford in Norfolk earned 18/- (90p) a week (an under-keeper might be paid 19/- (95p) a week at this time), with a free cottage worth £5 a year and firing valued at £2 per annum. A good trapper could expect to receive promotion to gamekeeper after several years' service on an estate. One keeper at Woburn Abbey in the nineteenth century began his career as rook trapper to the Duke of Bedford!

Warreners (on far left and far right wearing smocks) posing for the camera with a shooting party and a bag of rabbits on a Shropshire estate c1900.

Above left: Henry Grass (on right) head trapper to the 9th Duke of Rutland, at Belvoir Castle, Leicestershire, c1930. Responsible for the eradication of vermin over a 20,000 acre estate, he managed a team of three under-trappers, each of whom had his own beat.

Above right: Used by generations of trappers and gamekeepers to catch rabbits, rats, foxes and other species of ground vermin, the gin trap was banned in 1954 and replaced by more humane trapping methods.

The beater

Engaged on a part-time basis to drive the game birds towards the Guns at a driven shoot, the beater has been an integral part of the gamekeeping team on a shoot day since the practice of driven game shooting was introduced into Great Britain from Central Europe in the early nineteenth century. Until the mid-twentieth century, beaters (known as 'brushers' in certain parts of eastern England) were invariably estate workers who were redeployed from their day-to-day duties to assist on a shoot, or local farm hands who were keen to augment their wages during late autumn and winter when other work was scarce. Thereafter, landowners encountered a 'beater shortage' caused by a decline in the population in many rural areas, a 'knock-on' effect of the agricultural mechanisation that had taken place in the immediate post-war period. Many now started to recruit interested townsmen as well as countrymen to undertake beating duties, often providing an end of season beaters' shoot to encourage regular attendance on shoot days.

Beating has gradually changed beyond all recognition over the past fifty years or so and has become something of a social occasion rather than an opportunity for a farm worker to earn extra money to supplement low agricultural wages. Indeed, a modern beating team might easily include a car mechanic, a bank manager and a prosperous businessman, as well as two or three women, all of whom can shoot just as well as any of the Guns on the shooting field.

Today, beating on a driven game shoot is probably more popular than ever before, attracting men and women from all walks of life, even though remuneration is relatively modest, perhaps £25 to £40 a day with a cooked lunch and a couple of brace of pheasants or partridges to take home. Beaters now have their own professional

body, too, the National Organisation of Beaters and Pickers Up (founded in 2005 and commonly known as NOBS), which acts as an agency to provide beaters for shoots and represents their interests in countryside matters.

The loader

The loader, like the beater, is a part-time member of staff hired on a driven shoot day. His principal role is to replenish a sportsman's guns as quickly as possible to enable him to shoot at game birds continuously. In addition, he is responsible for cleaning the guns and for their security. He is invariably an extremely knowledgeable individual who can, if necessary, act as a mentor to a young or inexperienced shot, advising him or her on safe shooting procedures, shoot etiquette and general countryside matters.

Country landowners traditionally recruited loaders on an in-house basis either

Gamekeepers with a party of beaters on an estate near Hastings, East Sussex, c1900. The gamekeepers are dressed in a dark livery uniform, probably green or blue, while the beaters are wearing white smocks and caps. The small boys in similar attire were employed as stops.

from their household or their estate staff. The most popular candidates were a valet or an under-keeper, although it was not unknown for a suitable chauffeur, gardener or farm labourer to be asked to load. Often young, single men, they were expected to travel with their master wherever he went shooting, be it on his own estate or as an invited guest either at home or abroad. Those selected to act as loaders would, of course, if not from a gamekeeping background, receive appropriate training from the estate head gamekeeper.

Loading continued to be carried out in the time-honoured manner by gamekeepers and other servants until the 1970s and '80s. Thereafter, shoot owners, especially those operating commercial shoots, began to provide their own loaders for health and safety reasons, in order to have experienced men with an in-depth knowledge of the shooting field layout and to enable repeat clients to have their own regular loader, if required. Like beating, loading started to attract men and women from a variety of backgrounds and today loaders can range from retired gamekeepers, self-employed countryside craftsmen and 'lady loaders' who might earn from £50 to £100 a day, to professional men who load every Saturday in return for a couple of day's boundary shooting and an invitation to the end of season beaters' shoot.

Colonel Herbert Smith (seated talking to lady) with his loader standing behind on a Norfolk shoot, 1913.

3

THE HUNT ESTABLISHMENT

THE HUNT ESTABLISHMENT formed an integral part of almost every country estate of any stature during the eighteenth and the nineteenth centuries, with stabling for hunters, kennel facilities for hounds and harriers and accommodation for staff. Packs of hounds or harriers were kept in order to hunt foxes, hares, otters, polecats, rats or deer, both for pleasure and for pest control purposes. The landowner or a member of his family acted as the master of hounds, while the mounted followers might include friends, some of the more prosperous tenant farmers and the head gamekeeper. Each hunt had its own uniform, worn by the master and hunt servants when riding out in the field.

Nicknamed the 'Ancestor' by King Edward VII because of his dignified appearance, the 4th Lord Ribblesdale acted as joint-master of the Ribblesdale Buckhounds from 1906 until 1919 and as master from 1914 until the early 1920s. Kennelled at Gisburn Park near Clitheroe in Lancashire, the Ribblesdale family seat, the pack hunted wild deer in the Ribble Valley and over the surrounding moorlands.

Foxes preserved for sport at the expense of game birds

On estates where hunting took precedence over shooting, foxes were customarily preserved for sport at the expense of game birds rather than shot or trapped as vermin. In many instances the gamekeeping staff actively caught young foxes and cubs, rearing them on to maturity for release in areas where they were scarce. Landowners also purchased consignments of foxes from the Highlands of Scotland for the same reason.

Hunt staff releasing a 'bagged' or hand-reared fox on a West Country estate c1930.

Tenant farms on estates where hunting took place on a regular basis were generally let at a relatively low rental in times past in order to compensate the occupants for any damage carried out by the horses and hounds when running over cultivated land. Some hunts also operated a poultry fund, which compensated farmers for the loss of poultry killed by foxes, and a wire fund to pay for repairs to damaged fencing. In return for these benefits, tenant farmers were expected to undertake puppy-walking duties for the hunt and to carry out earth stopping on their land if required.

Prestigious hunts

The great majority of the more prestigious estate hunts, such as the Beaufort, the Belvoir, the Portman and the Wilton, continue to operate today, although all are now run by a committee that appoints the master and hunt servants, rely upon subscriptions and the fundraising activities of a supporters' club for their income, and depend upon the goodwill of landowners and farmers for access to hunting country. Many of the smaller hunting establishments belonging to impoverished noblemen and country squires were disbanded during the late Victorian period due to rising costs, loss of country, or fox and hare shortages caused by over-hunting by some of the larger packs of hounds and harriers. Some lingered on into the 1920s and '30s, often as unregistered packs, but few have survived until the present time.

Fox 'mask' preserved and mounted on a wooden shield. It was something of a tradition among masters of hounds and hunt servants in times past to 'preserve' the heads and brushes (tails) of foxes that had been taken after a notable run or in an unusual location.

Earl Fitzwilliam's hunt establishment

Hunting enthusiast the 7th Earl Fitzwilliam owned and financed three prestigious packs of foxhounds during the Edwardian period: Lord Fitzwilliam's and Island (in Ireland), Earl Fitzwilliam's (Grove) and Earl Fitzwilliam's (Wentworth). The latter pack was kennelled at his principal seat, Wentworth Woodhouse in the West Riding of Yorkshire, the largest private house in Great Britain. In addition to hunting over an extensive area of the surrounding countryside, the pack hunted regularly on the 15,000 acre Wentworth Woodhouse estate where, according to a contemporary magazine, foxes were 'positively venerated' and 'bred in large numbers yearly'.

Meet of Earl Fitzwilliam's (Wentworth) Foxhounds outside Wentworth Woodhouse c1907.

The entry for the Wentworth pack in the 1908–9 edition of *Baily's Hunting Directory* states:

Earl Fitzwilliam's (Wentworth)
Distinctive collar – Green, plain silver buttons. Evening dress – Red, dark green velvet collar, white facings, white waistcoat, silver buttons. Master – (1902) Earl Fitzwilliam, Wentworth Woodhouse, Rotherham. Secretary of Wire and Poultry Funds – G.A. Wilson Esq., Butterthwaite, near Sheffield. Huntsman – (1907) Sam Morgan. Whippers-in – 1st (1908) H. Tyrell; 2nd (1907) Harry Trueman. 25 couples of hounds tattooed 'F' and litter number right ear. Kennels –

continued overleaf

Wentworth. Telegraph Office – Wentworth. Station – Rotherham, 4
miles. Days of Meeting – Two a week.
The country, which lies in Yorks. and Derbyshire, is about 20 miles in
greatest width E. to W. and 15 miles N. to S. On the N. it adjoins the
Badsworth; on the W. the country is not hunted; on the S. it adjoins
the Barlow, and on the E. Earl Fitzwilliam's (Grove). All sorts of fences
are encountered, both ditch and wall, also rough fences on banks on
the Derbyshire side. It consists of about equal parts of pasture and
plough, with large woods on the Doncaster side. The wire is taken
down during the season and replaced in spring by the Wire Committee.
A thoroughbred is the horse required. Best centres; Rotherham, about
the middle of the country; Sheffield, whence meets of the Barlow, and
Doncaster, on the Badsworth border, whence meets of Earl Fitzwilliam's
(Grove) can be reached.
A private pack owned by the Master, who defrays all expenses save
those met by the Wire and Poultry Funds. No Cap.

The servants employed in a hunt establishment, commonly referred to as 'hunt servants', are directly accountable to the master of hounds and do not form a part of the stables staff on a country estate. Under the day-to-day command of the huntsman, the team includes at least one whipper-in and one kennelman, depending upon the number of hounds or harriers kept.

A trio of perfectly turned out hunt servants c1910.

The huntsman

The key servant in every hunt establishment, the huntsman not only hunts the hounds or harriers and is responsible for controlling the pack on the field and for 'finding' the quarry, but is also in charge of the kennels and general hound welfare. He must have an intimate knowledge of the country being hunted over and the ability to get on well with the local farmers and gamekeepers.

Huntsmen have always been held in high esteem in the countryside by lord and labourer alike and traditionally commanded far more respect from ordinary folk than members of the gamekeeping fraternity, who were often disliked. Indeed, during the second half of the nineteenth century, the huntsmen of the Belvoir, the Quorn, the Pytchley and other packs in the English shires had a near God-like status within the local community. That said, it was not always easy to find a really talented huntsman at this time according to the well-known Victorian master of hounds, Henry Chaplin (later 1st Viscount Chaplin), who, in the 1860s wrote: 'I have often said it was easier to find a good Prime Minister than a real good huntsman, and Heaven knows that either is difficult enough.'

On some of the smaller 'all-round' country estates during the late eighteenth and the nineteenth centuries it was not uncommon for the head gamekeeper to double as huntsman of a small pack of hounds and harriers. For example, at Herriard Park in North Hampshire, James Hibberd, head keeper to Colonel George Purefoy Jervoise, M.P., from 1797 until 1817, hunted his master's private pack of harriers, which were kept to control hares and foxes on the property. In addition to his annual salary of £42 as keeper, he was paid a supplement of £3-3/- (£3.15) as huntsman, plus a free house, a domestic servant, a free uniform, fuel and an allowance of 3/- (15p) a week for keep of a cow and 2d (1p) a week for the keep of a pointer and a spaniel. His 'Kennel Account' for 1805 includes payments of £42-10/-10d (£42.54) for a years' supply of barley for the harriers, 4/- (20p) for a physician 'to look at the dogs', and £1-1/- (£1.05) for the purchase of a hound puppy from Mr Portal of Freefolk. In 1811, the 'Account' goes as far as to note that the harriers consumed the flesh of nine horses, two cows, one sheep and forty-six lambs, the total cost of which amounted to £13.

Huntsman in full regalia c1900.

Jack West, kennel huntsman of the Bentley Harriers in Worcestershire, c1892. Owned by Maude Cheape, the 'lady squire' of Bentley, the pack was kennelled at Bentley Manor and hunted on and around the Bentley estate.

The kennel huntsman

In circumstances where the master hunts the hounds or harriers personally, a kennel huntsman is employed to manage the kennels, to supervise feeding and exercising activities and to act as a whipper-in on the field.

The whipper-in

Effectively an assistant huntsman, the whipper-in keeps a pack of hounds together on the field and rounds up any that have strayed. He also helps with the general care of the hounds in the kennels. Most hunts have two whippers-in, known respectively as the first whipper-in and the second whipper-in.

Many of the private packs of hounds and harriers that operated on less prestigious country estates during the nineteenth and the early twentieth centuries did not retain a full-time whipper-in but enlisted a groom from the stables or an under-gamekeeper to perform the role as and when required. Sir Lewes Loveden Pryse, Bt., Master of the Goggerdan Hunt in Cardiganshire from 1919 until 1946, appointed a rather novel dual-purpose whipper-in, Ceredig Davies, who acted as butler during the evenings and cooked breakfast after an early morning hunt, as well as accompanying his master on his annual fishing trip to the Shetland Islands as his ghillie!

The groom

Similar in status to the groom employed in the stables to look after the carriage and riding horses, the hunt groom is responsible for the hunting horses kept at the kennels. In a large hunt establishment, a stud groom is retained who not only supervises a small team of grooms, but is also involved in horse breaking and, possibly, horse breeding.

The second horseman

Usually a groom, the second horseman accompanies his master on the hunting field, lightly riding a 'back-up' horse from point to point during the morning then changing horses with his master during the middle of the day, thus enabling him to have a fresh horse for the afternoon. Few hunting folk retain a second horseman today or have two hunters out on the field due to the costs involved.

Left: Lady riding side-saddle at a meet of hounds on an immaculately turned out hunter, prepared and saddled up by a groom.

Below (top): Kennelman with hounds at the Grafton Hunt kennels, Paulerspury, Northamptonshire 1911.

Below (middle): Hounds on parade at an unknown hunt kennels c1925.

Below (bottom): Invitation to the West Warwickshire Farmers Foxhounds annual Earth Stoppers Supper 1973.

The kennelman

The hunt servant responsible for feeding and exercising a pack of hounds or harriers, his duties also include skinning and butchering cattle carcases to feed to the hounds and acting as cook. In times past, many of the more prestigious private hunt establishments employed several kennelmen as well as one or two kennel boys to assist them. Kennel boys often progressed up the 'hunting ladder' to become whips or even huntsmen.

The earth stopper

A man retained by a hunt to 'stop' or block fox earths and badger setts (the latter activity was banned in 1992 following the passage of the Badgers Act) in a particular area prior to a meet of hounds taking place in order to prevent foxes from going to ground. Traditionally carried out by gamekeepers, woodmen and other estate staff or by tenant farmers, who were all paid a fee for each fox found on their 'patch', earth stopping is now usually undertaken by professional hunt terriermen. Earth stopping payments are generally made at the annual earth stoppers' supper, a sumptuous dinner held by many packs of fox hounds at the end of the hunting season.

THE JOINT MASTERS OF THE
WEST WARWICKSHIRE FARMERS FOXHOUNDS

cordially invite you to the

EARTH-STOPPERS SUPPER

at the

WILDMOOR HOTEL · STRATFORD-on-AVON

TUESDAY 26th JUNE 1973

7.30 p.m. for 8.00 p.m.

Top: The Culmstock Otter Hounds in action c1901.

Bottom: Exmoor squire, Henry Grey Thornton, author of the hunt records, with a catch of fish taken on his Scottish estate c1930.

Hunt Records

In more leisurely days, many hunting folk kept detailed diaries recording epic runs, notable 'finds', companions in the field and anecdotes about hunt servants for posterity. Excerpts from the journal of Exmoor Squire Henry Grey Thornton, who served variously as Master of the Culmstock Otter Hounds and Deputy-Master of the Devon & Somerset Staghounds, give a brief account of four meets that he attended in 1901:

4th March, Devon and Somerset staghounds at Hawkridge
Found 2 hinds and hunted round Molland Moor, Withypool Common and Hawkridge and laid pack in near Tarr Steps. Continued down to Three Waters and Mr Amory's side to Chilly Bridge then onto the weir and Haddon Water, and back to the weir and killed a hind. A very good run and a hard day for horses, one of the best I have had.

7th August, Culmstock Otter hounds at Chain Bridge
Worked up to junction of rivers and found on Little Exe after 1 hour, 50 minutes. Killed a large dog otter of 27lbs. after a capital hunt.

19th September, Devon & Somerset Staghounds at Heath Poult Cross
Found near Luxborough and ran by Dunster towards Minehead and killed an 11-pointer stag under the new pier. 18-mile ride home.

2nd November, Dulverton Foxhounds at Rhyll Manor
Opening Meet. Champagne breakfast. Ran 2 foxes but did not kill. Scent poor. Very good spread indeed at the breakfast.

4

THE RIVER KEEPER

RIVER KEEPING AS a specialist profession dates back to the first half of the nineteenth century when country landowners began to let out salmon and trout fishing rights to professional gentlemen from major towns and cities, many of whom formed clubs to rent or lease stretches of water. Prior to this time rivers were looked after by estate gamekeepers, who usually did little more than keep poachers at bay.

    The first dedicated river keepers (sometimes also known as water keepers) were often employed by angling tenants rather than by landowners and were not only expected to carry out poaching prevention duties and basic management tasks such as vermin control, weed cutting and hatch maintenance but also to attend anglers

John Cragg fishing on Webbs Pool on the river Test at Broadlands c1900. The first river keeper on the estate, he was appointed in 1881 and retired in 1905.

when out fishing. Usually from a gamekeeping background, these men tended to be recruited from out of the area so they were not familiar with members of the local poaching fraternity or the river owner and would not allow the owner or his friends to illicitly fish a river in the absence of the tenants!

On the river Test in Hampshire, for example, the Stockbridge-based Houghton Fishing Club, who leased a long section of the Middle Test, appear to have engaged a couple of river keepers shortly after its formation in 1822. Lower down the Test, on the Broadlands estate at Romsey, the owner, Lord Mount Temple chose to employ an in-house keeper, John Cragg, after deciding to let out the salmon and trout fishing rights to a syndicate of three anglers in 1881.

The late Victorian period

By the late Victorian period, river keepers could be found on most private estates with good river fishings, irrespective of whether or not the owner let out the fishing rights or reserved them for himself and his friends. If the fishings were retained 'in hand', the keeper would come under the control of the head gamekeeper and would usually be expected to carry out loading or beating duties on a shoot day. On some properties, an under-keeper even doubled as a river keeper and combined pheasant rearing with fish preservation!

River keeping, like gamekeeping, had now started to become a highly specialised profession. Keepers were expected to embrace the latest river management techniques to ensure a good stock of fish on their water, restocking with trout on a regular basis or introducing additional quarry species such as the Loch Leven trout, which were said to fight better. As well as carrying out vermin control and weed clearance duties, keepers were often responsible for cutting back trees and undergrowth adjacent to the river bank for ease of back-casting, mowing the banks with scythes for access purposes, building seats and shelters for the comfort of anglers and, if any water meadows were in the vicinity, liaising with the local 'drowners' in order that the meadows were managed in the best interests of the fishery. If commercial salmon netting took place, particularly on the tidal lower reaches of a river, they would invariably keep a 'watching brief' to make sure that operations were carried out legally.

Skilled angling instructors

Many river keepers became skilled angling instructors, teaching young gentlemen how to fish correctly, and were accomplished fly tiers. It was not unusual for them to perform the role of ghillie for their employer or his guests. Further, they would normally clean, pack and dispatch any fish not required for household use to a local fishmonger or game dealer.

Estate river keepers were paid at a similar rate to under-gamekeepers and were provided with a free house, free fuel, a suit of clothes of clothes annually and, if lucky enough, were allowed a supply of rabbits and fish for the table. If employed by an angling tenant, a fishing syndicate or a club, they might receive a higher salary as well as the usual perks and profit from cash tips given by visiting fishermen.

World War One

River keeping operations suffered a severe blow when World War One was declared in 1914. Many young keepers enlisted in the services to fight for their country, leaving large stretches of river neglected. Other than on club waters, where elderly members often acted as volunteer keepers, banks fell into disrepair and fish stocks were depleted through heavy poaching. Some patriotic landowners did not help matters by regularly netting salmon and trout to help the war effort by supplying food to local towns!

Following the cessation of hostilities in 1918 many landowners were forced to make economies due to high taxation and death duties, with the result that river fishing rights on private estates throughout the country were either sold off to private buyers or angling clubs and syndicates, or leased out to long-term tenants who were responsible for the maintenance of the fishings. River keeping now became the responsibility of independent riparian owners or lessees who employed stand alone keepers and watchers to protect their interests. Thereafter, few estates continued to employ an in-house river keeper.

Walter Hurst, river and gamekeeper to Colonel William Cornwallis-West at Ruthin Castle, Denbighshire. during the second half of the nineteenth century. A skilled angling instructor, he taught the art of fishing with worm and fly to his employer's children, Major George Cornwallis-West, the noted angling author, and Shelagh, 2nd Duchess of Westminster.

Rivers fared better during World War Two than during the previous conflict. Keepers were generally exempted from military service in order to carry out vermin control in the countryside, which enabled them to undertake their duties on a part-time basis with the assistance of pensioner helpers. Some served with the Home Guard, too, and could usually manage to combine night patrolling with river watching.

The post-World War Two era

Since the end of World War Two, river keeping has undergone many changes in order to survive into the twenty-first century. Private landowners with river fishings and independent riparian proprietors have been obliged for economic reasons to provide day ticket angling facilities for members of the public, with

the result that some keepers have become involved with marketing the fishery and selling tickets. Large urban-based coarse fishing clubs have purchased or leased river beats to enable their members to fish for salmon or trout and have introduced volunteer river keepers to look after their waters to augment the paid staff. Further, many keepers now regularly undertake angling tuition and public relations work such as guided walks and talk about their work to various organisations on a regular basis. Last but not least, since the 1970s a number of countryside colleges have provided full-time river keeping and fishery management courses to enable students to train as professional keepers.

Anticlockwise from top left:
Bert Tiller, head gamekeeper on the Broadlands estate, Hampshire, c1935. An accomplished angler, he not only ran the shoot but was also responsible for maintaining the Broadlands section of the river Test, which was managed by an in-house river keeper on his staff. *Courtesy of B. Whittle*

Walter Geary (on right), in-house river keeper at Broadlands from 1913 until 1964, pictured here with Captain Frisby and a catch of ten salmon taken from the river Test on 2 and 3 June 1928.

River keeper (on left) and angler posing for the camera with a large salmon landed from the river Wye in Herefordshire …

… and (on right) in the process of placing the fish in a carrying basket after weighing had been completed. Both photographs c1955.

5

THE PARK KEEPER

THE PARK OR deer park keeper was one of the principal outdoor servants on the larger English country estates from the late seventeenth century until the outbreak of World War One. His main function was to manage the herds of deer – red, roe or fallow or a mixture of all three – that roamed over the wooded parklands surrounding many castles, mansions and manor houses. He often served as park bailiff, too, taking charge of the pigs, cattle and horses kept in the park by local cottagers on an 'agistment' or fee-paying basis, and issuing permits authorising poor people to collect firewood, blackberries or nuts on specified dates.

Responsible directly to the head gamekeeper on an estate, the park keeper held a higher status to that of a senior beat keeper. He was paid a higher salary and frequently received all or part of the proceeds of venison sales as part of his emoluments. If a park keeper was not employed on a property, it was usual for the head gamekeeper to undertake deer management duties in return for a bonus payment.

Pay and perks

In 1866, the agent to the 5th Duke of Portland at Welbeck Abbey in Nottinghamshire carried out a comparative study of park keepers' wages in order to establish whether or not the Welbeck park keeper, James Boaler, who received an annual salary of £80 with a 'present' of £20, was being overpaid. He found that at Woburn Abbey the Duke of Bedford paid his park keeper £30 per annum along with fees arising from the sale of venison, a free house, a supply of coal worth £8, powder and shot worth £2, clothes to the value of £15, a horse for transport, and keep for two cows. At Chatsworth the Duke of Devonshire paid his park keeper £100 a year but expected him to provide his own house and horse, and to pay rent to the estate for pasturage for his cows. While at Belvoir Castle and Thoresby Park the Duke of Rutland and Earl Manvers both gave their respective park keepers an annual salary of £55-10/- (£55.50) together with a house, garden and pasturage valued at £38, with the men being responsible for providing their own horse and ammunition.

Opposite: Park keeper feeding deer at Wentworth Woodhouse, South Yorkshire, c1906.

The deer park

Deer parks date back to the Norman period when large tracts of land were enclosed with high fences or walls by the nobility and gentry in order to hold deer for hunting purposes and to provide venison for the table. Many of these parks survived until the declaration of the Commonwealth in 1649 when the Cromwellian forces gradually destroyed parks, one by one, butchering the deer or releasing the herds into the wild. Following the restoration of the monarchy in 1660, members of the aristocracy and

the landed gentry began to recreate deer parks on private estates. By 1900, the number of deer parks in England stood at around 395, the most prestigious being at Windsor, Tatton, Eastwell, Grimthorpe, Thoresby and Blenheim. Deer parks at this time were exempted from the annual tithe payment levied by the Church of England on the proviso that the ground was not ploughed up or the herds of deer killed or removed.

Sadly, the outbreak of World War One signalled the end of the deer park on numerous great estates after the Prime Minister, Lloyd George, imposed a tax on the parks to help pay for the war effort. Although the tax was short lived, landowners were forced to slaughter entirely or decimate their herds of deer due to severe food shortages and restrictions. The cleft oak fences that were a feature of nearly all the parks fell into disrepair as estate woodmen were called up to fight. When the hostilities ceased, with the exception of a small number of major landowners, few people bothered either to repair the fences or replace their, deer resulting in the loss of such parks throughout the country.

Inevitably, those deer parks that managed to survive the vicissitudes of the war years had severely depleted herds that needed to be rebuilt, a time-consuming and a costly process that took a decade or more to complete. Few dedicated deer park keepers were employed at this time for reasons of economy, with ordinary gamekeepers looking after the herds of deer on many estates in addition to their normal duties.

Left: Fallow deer in the 700 acre deer park at Petworth House, West Sussex – home of England's largest and oldest herd of fallow deer. *Courtesy of C.G. Hallam*

Below: Deer shooting party with the day's bag at Ugbrooke Park, Devon, c1939.

English country house deer parks were dealt a further blow following the declaration of World War Two when landowners were obliged to reduce their herds to provide food for people in towns and cities. At Wentworth Woodhouse in Yorkshire, the herd of deer was reduced from 300 to thirty between 1939 and 1945 through culling and poaching, although a dedicated park keeper continued to be retained. On the Ugbrooke Park estate in Devon, Lord Clifford of Chudleigh was forced to cull the bulk of his herd of deer. However, at Woburn Abbey, the 12th Duke of Bedford deliberately broke the law, refusing to accept a reduction in his deer and bison herds, as well as diverting vast quantities of animal fodder from his farms to feed them. Although his actions were considered unpatriotic at the time, they did ensure the survival of the Père David's deer, which was then on the verge of extinction.

Some of the more enterprising landowners revitalised their deer parks in the wake of the war, promoting them as a tourist attraction if they opened their stately home to the public. Indeed, the stately home 'revolution' undoubtedly ensured the survival of a number of deer parks until the present time. According to recent estimates, between seventy and eighty deer parks remain in England today.

Ornamental cattle in deer parks

It was not uncommon for landowners during the late Victorian and the Edwardian periods to keep a herd of ornamental cattle in their park in addition to the deer to add variety to the stock. Looked after by the park keeper, the most popular breeds were white park cattle, descendants of the wild cattle that once roamed throughout the British Isles, and Highland cattle. George Assheton-Smith, owner of Vaynol Park estate in Caernarvonshire from 1869 until 1904, kept both white park cattle and American bison, the latter breeding freely alongside the cattle and deer in his park. Today, white park cattle are something or a rarity but herds continue to survive at Chillingham in Northumberland, Cadzow in Lanarkshire, Dynevor Castle in Carmarthenshire and in a few other places.

Highland cattle in the deer park at Wentworth Woodhouse, South Yorkshire, c1906.

Deer herd management

The park keeper was traditionally responsible for feeding deer, protecting them from the predations of poachers, culling and butchering aged and malformed beasts and distributing venison to favoured 'giveaways' and game dealers. He might also exchange stags or bucks with other deer parks on an annual basis for stock improvement purposes, or purchase 'stock' deer from dealers for the same reason. More often than not a park keeper lived in a lodge within the confines of a deer park in order that he could keep an eye on his charges at all times.

On a large country estate with an extensive deer park, the park keeper often looked after herds of red, roe or fallow deer, numbering perhaps between 300 and 2,000 head. As an example, in 1837, the Duke of Beaufort's park keeper at Badminton in Gloucestershire cared for 1,400 fallow deer and 400 red deer As a further example, in 1912, the park keeper at Rushmore House in Wiltshire managed 400 head of deer, consisting of herds of red, roe, fallow and Japanese (sika) deer.

Today, the park keeper is something of a rare species, found only on a small number of estates, although active deer management is carried out by gamekeepers, stalkers and others in virtually all the historic deer parks that have survived into the twenty-first century.

Billy Archer, park keeper to the 10th Lord Middleton at Wollaton Hall, Nottinghamshire, with a 'grassed' or dead red deer stag c1920.

6

THE STABLES STAFF

MANAGED BY THE head coachman, the stables staff provided all the transport facilities required by the owner of a country estate, caring for the carriage and the riding horses and maintaining the fleet of horse-drawn vehicles used for long- and short-haul journeys, conveying Guns to the shooting field and transporting goods. Based in the stable block, generally a large imposing complex of buildings situated a short distance away from the mansion, the coachmen, grooms, stable helpers, stable boys and other staff members lived on site in dormitories or single rooms above the main offices, depending upon their seniority. They either cooked and ate their meals in an adjacent kitchen-mess room or dined in the servants' hall. The staff worked long hours, rising at 4 or 5 a.m. in summer and 6 a.m. in wintertime, and could expect to finish late in the evening if their master or a member of his family had gone out to dinner or to attend a ball. It goes without saying, of course, that anyone employed in the stables needed to be able to handle and ride a horse correctly!

Above: View of part of the stable block on the Tilgate estate, West Sussex, c1920.

Opposite: Tom Jones, personal coachman to Sir Charles Philipps, Bt., at Picton Castle, Pembrokeshire, 1904.

List of stables staff employed by the 8th Duke of Beaufort at Badminton Park, Gloucestershire in 1836:

1 Head Groom
1 Coachman
1 Second Coachman
2 Postillions
1 Pad Groom
33 Stablemen and Helpers
1 Carriage Washer

Total number of Carriage Horses, Hunters, Hacks, Ponies etc. in stables: **119**

The head coachman

The man in charge of the stables staff, the head coachman was effectively the transport manager on a country estate, being responsible for all the horses – other than those used in the hunt establishment or on the home farm – and all the coaches, carriages, traps and assorted horse-drawn conveyances. Normally accountable to the land agent, he either lived in an apartment in the stable block or in a nearby house. In addition to his salary, which varied according to the size of the establishment and the number of staff beneath him, he was provided with free fuel and supplied with two livery uniforms and two stable suits annually, together with two hats, two pairs of boots and a box coat. If employed by royalty, a nobleman or a senior military officer, he wore a cockade in his hat to denote his status, along with silver or brass buttons bearing his master's crest on his coat and livery uniform. He was, nevertheless, a 'hands-on' employee and personally drove and maintained the best coach in the fleet, as well as caring for the pair of horses used to pull it.

Samuel and Sarah Adams, writing *The Complete Servant* in 1825, have this to say about the head coachman's position in the outdoor service hierarchy and the duties expected of him:

> On the sobriety, steady conduct, and respectable appearance of this important servant, depend the exterior appearance of the family with which he resides. Every genuine coachman has his characteristic costume. His flaxen curls or wig, his low cocked hat, his plush breeches, and his Benjamin surtout, his clothes also being well brushed, and the lace and buttons in a state of high polish. Care in driving his horses so as to preserve his own family and not to injure other passengers on horse or foot, so that he may not involve his master in law-suits, and wound the feelings of those he is driving, is of the utmost consequence. It is his business to have the carriages kept in repair, and to prevent his master being imposed upon by wanton charges; and in like manner to advise and assist in the purchase of horses, and in this delicate business, protect the interest of his employer. Much depends on his zeal, as to the annual expenditure of a carriage, with reference to the coachmaker, the horse-dealer and the farrier; and he will do well always to make special contract, and leave as little as possible to the conscience of others. When only one coachman is kept, his duties generally include the whole of the stable business, as well as the cleaning, greasing, and examining the carriage; he should never trust to chance and consult the smith or coachmaker as often as he apprehends a possibility of danger.

The second, personal or lady's coachman

Immediately below the head coachman in the stables staff hierarchy, the second coachman, known otherwise as the personal or the lady's coachman, was responsible for the second-best coach in the coach house and the corresponding horses. He undertook all the night driving duties required by his employer, using the second-best equipage, and drove his master or mistress on short personal journeys in a light carriage or a trap. In some less affluent establishments he not only accompanied the family to London for the season, driving them around town on private visits or on business, but acted as a postillion or as a courier.

The under coachman

Usually a young man, the under-coachman maintained and drove the less prestigious coaches and carriages, traps and other horse-drawn vehicles kept in the stables complex to transport his employer, family members and guests in and around a country estate. In addition, he collected supplies for the mansion from the nearest town or railway station, drove senior servants on work-related journeys and might drive a shooting brake whenever a large shooting party took place. Some landowners employed two or three coachmen in pre-motor car days, each of whom had one of the inferior coaches or carriages in their care.

The groom

Considered to be inferior in rank to the coachmen in days gone by, the groom was nevertheless one of the most important servants in the stables and was responsible for ensuring that the carriage and riding horses were kept in the peak of condition at all times, and that the saddlery and tackle was maintained to a high standard. His duties included feeding and grooming the horses, mucking them out, exercising them on a regular basis, bedding them down at night and

Under coachman dressed in livery uniform driving a pony and trap c1910.

63

Above: Immaculately groomed horse saddled up and awaiting a rider c1910.

Right: Groom on exercise duty in snowy conditions on the Westbury Manor estate, Buckinghamshire, 1906.

putting them on parade for inspection in the stableyard in the morning, if requested by his master. He accompanied his master or mistress on horseback when out riding and, if a really proficient horseman, was expected to teach their children how to ride properly. The stables at a large establishment would have a head groom, otherwise known as a stable master, who controlled a team of grooms, helpers and stable boys. However, if the stables were small, it was not unknown for a groom to double as a valet or a footman in the absence of other available staff!

The pad groom

The pad groom escorted his master or mistress when out riding, travelling by foot rather than on horseback. He was often a groom of long standing who was redeployed from his normal duties for the purpose as and when required.

The footman

Essentially a member of the household staff rather than an outdoor servant, the footman nevertheless worked alongside the coachman and other members of the stables team on a fairly regular basis. If he was on 'carriage duty', he would sit next to the coachman on an enclosed coach or carriage whenever his master and mistress were travelling, or, alternatively, perch on a 'dicky seat' attached to the rear of an open carriage or other conveyance. In addition to helping them in and out of the vehicle and providing them with rugs, hot water bottles and umbrellas according to the weather, he would blow a whistle to warn lodge or toll house keepers to open the gates in advance of their arrival. He might also accompany his mistress when out making calls during the afternoon, announcing her visit at the hostess's house and escorting her on and off the premises, or act as a 'greeter' at a railway station, meeting guests off a train and leading them to an awaiting coach or carriage outside. Important journeys, such as state or civic occasions, necessitated the use of two footmen, both of whom would either sit on the 'dicky seat' or stand upright on a small platform at the back of a coach or carriage dressed in full livery uniform.

Footman in household dress, 1914. The footman in a large country house could expect to spend time on carriage duty, usually during the afternoon, in addition to carrying out his normal duties.

The postillion

Rarely a full-time occupation other than on a prestigious country estate with a large fleet of coaches, carriages and other horse-drawn vehicles, the postillion doubled either as a groom or a senior stable boy who was proficient in horsemanship. His job entailed riding the left or 'near' horse of a pair of horses drawing a carriage, effectively acting as the driver (the coachman would be mounted on the vehicle together with the passengers). If a coach or a carriage required two pairs of horses to pull it, there would be two postillions, one for each pair or, alternatively, one postillion would ride on the left-hand rear horse in order to control all four horses. In the case of a long journey, a land owner would use his own postillions and horses as far as the first posting house (usually a coaching inn) then hire fresh postillions and horses at each additional posting house to convey his carriage onwards through each 'stage' (a section of the route) until he reached his final destination, a mode of travel known as 'posting'. Unlike a groom, who wore a frock coat and riding attire, the postillion dressed in a uniform consisting of a jacket and a cap, along with a special rigid boot on his right leg that provided protection against being crushed by the central wooden shaft of a carriage (if any) or the body of the adjacent horse.

The courier or outrider

The courier or outrider accompanied a landowner and his family when undertaking a long journey by carriage or coach. Usually an under-coachman, a groom or a footman redeployed from his normal duties, he not only acted as guard (often armed) in order to protect his charges from the predations of highwaymen, but also rode ahead as and when required to pay turnpike fees, to request refreshments at wayside inns and to make arrangements at coaching inns where the party proposed to stay for the night. Important for ensuring a safe and smooth journey prior to the coming of the railways in the early Victorian period, the courier had become obsolete by the late nineteenth century after the train had replaced horse-drawn transport as the principal mode of travel and the turnpike road system had been disbanded.

Coach Travel – the Georgian way

John Archer, a wealthy landed gentleman with estates in various parts of England, made an annual progress around his properties during the late eighteenth century, transporting his household and valuables in a retinue of carriages accompanied by his stables staff, hunt servants and other employees. An anonymous observer, writing under the pseudonym of 'An Amateur Sportsman' in Sporting Anecdotes: Original and Select in 1804 provides a detailed description of this spectacle:

> The style in which Mr Archer travelled once a year when he visited his estates, resembled more the pompous pageantry of the ancient nobles of Spain, when they went to take possession of a vice-royalty, than that of a plain country gentleman. The following was the order of the cavalcade:- 1st. the coach and six horses, with two postillions and coachman. Three out-riders. Post-chaise and four post-horses. Phaeton and four horses, followed by two grooms. A chaise-marine with four horses, carrying the numerous services of plate. This last was escorted by the under-butler, who had under his command three stout fellows; they formed a part of the household; all were armed with blunderbusses. Next followed the hunters with their clothes on, of scarlet, trimmed with silver, attended by the stud-grooms and huntsman. Each horse has a fox's brush tied to the front of the bridle. The rear was brought up by the pack of hounds, the whipper-in, the hack horses, and the inferior stablemen. In the chariot Mrs Archer; or, if she preferred a less confined view of the country, she accompanied Mr Archer in the phaeton, who travelled in all weathers in that vehicle, wrapped up in a swansdown coat.

The stable helper

Known otherwise as the stableman, the strapper or the stable hand, the stable helper was in effect a 'jack of all trades' who worked beneath the grooms and the coachmen. According to Samuel and Sarah Adams, writing in The Complete Servant in 1825:

The helpers are subordinate to the regular stable servants, and their business is to assist in cleaning the horses, harness, saddles, and carriages, cleaning out the stables, and assisting the coachman and groom in all the business of the stable that may be required of them. They are generally hired by the week, at from 16 (80p) to 21 (£1.05) shillings, out of doors, and have no liveries. If hired as regular stable servants, they are boarded in the house, and their wages and clothing are nearly the same as the groom's.

The stable boy

Sometimes as young as ten years' of age prior to the introduction of compulsory education in 1870, the stable boy assisted the coachmen, the grooms and the stable helpers with their duties as and when required and might also ride as a postillion if needed. If he showed an aptitude for horsemanship, he could expect to be promoted to a groom or an under-coachman after several years of service. A full-time member of staff, he lived in a dormitory in the stables complex, his board and clothing being provided free of charge as part of his emoluments.

Mr O'Mara, a postillion employed in the Royal Mews at Buckingham Palace, seated on Cream, one of the King's horses, while driving a carriage c1930.

7

THE CHAUFFEUR

THE SUCCESSOR OF the coachman, the first chauffeurs began to appear at the tail end of the Victorian period when wealthy country landowners started to purchase motor cars for pleasure purposes. They were usually qualified mechanical engineers and were supplied by car manufacturers as driver–mechanics whenever a new vehicle was sold. Many were French or German rather than British, the great majority of early motor cars being manufactured in France or Germany and imported into Great Britain. The title chauffeur, in fact, is derived from the French noun for 'stoker', as some of the first French cars were powered by steam prior to the introduction of the internal combustion engine.

Notwithstanding the advantages of employing a factory-trained driver–mechanic as a chauffeur, members of the landed gentry and the aristocracy often selected an existing outdoor servant for the role, either sending him away to a motor manufacturer to learn how to drive and gain mechanical knowledge after ordering a new car, or instructing a company driver supplied with a car to provide him with 'on the job' training for a couple of weeks before placing him in charge of the car. Unlike a factory driver who was used to working for a set number of hours, a chauffeur recruited from the estate staff was conversant with the ways of the household and was used to being at his employer's beck and call as and when required, whatever the time of the day!

'Home-grown' chauffeurs

'Home-grown' chauffeurs tended to be young grooms or coachmen who not only saw it as something of a challenge to take charge of a 'horse-less carriage', but also as a promotion within the estate hierarchy. Gardeners, gamekeepers, footmen and other servants were chosen for the task, too, in some instances so that they could act as a relief driver on long journeys.

Opposite: Chauffeur driving an Armstrong Whitworth motor car, 1910.

Selecting a chauffeur

Claudine Murray, writing in the 1950s, recounts how her father, a Northumberland landowner, purchased a motor car in 1898, appointed a chauffeur from his estate staff and how the car subsequently arrived at the family home:

My father owned the first motor car in Northumberland. Although he had no mechanical bent, he took a scientist's interest in any new invention. Somewhere he came across an advertisement of a 'wagonette motor car' for sale at the Daimler works in Coventry. The engine had been designed for a yacht, but later adapted for a car. Straightaway his mind was made up: he would buy the car.

The question of a driver was easily solved. Our gamekeeper, a hill-bred Northumbrian, scion of a long line of keepers, had at some time in his youth and for a few months driven a light railway engine on a small local line. In the eyes of the whole family (and certainly in his own) he was therefore an engineer, fully competent to tackle the new internal combustion engine. So Charlton was dispatched by train to spend a few days at the Daimler works acquiring a complete knowledge of cars. He was then to drive back to Northumberland the 4hp Daimler, capable of a speed of 16mph on the level and of anything its momentum could attain downhill when released from brake and engine.

The whole family assembled at the front door to see the arrival of the new wonder. A loud chugging announced its approach through the park. Someone ran to open the gate which led to the gravel sweep, and through it proudly came Charlton perched aloft in the driving seat almost on top of the bonnet, steering with a 'tiller' shaped like the handle of an old-fashioned gramophone. The body was that of an open wagonette with the two facing seats set lengthwise and backed by padded rails; each took three people and the driver was in front. It stood high above the wheels, which had solid rubber tyres, and was entered by two steps up to the door at the back. There was of course no protection from the weather: when it was wet we used umbrellas. The registration number was, so far as I can remember, X1.

Essentially seen as outdoor servants, the early chauffeurs nevertheless did not fit in easily with the rigid staff hierarchy found on many country estates. On some properties they were accountable to the land agent, on others they reported directly to the landowner or, occasionally, came under the control of the house steward or butler and were considered to be indoor staff. Indeed, as the unknown chauffeur–author of *The Chauffeur's Blue Book* commented in 1906: 'We chauffeurs, you know, are a class and type of men that have never existed before. There are no recognised customs and rules of our order. We have not been brought up to our work, and we have nobody to guide our general conduct.'

The Royal example

The number of chauffeurs employed in Great Britain increased dramatically from 1900 onwards after King Edward VII bought a Daimler motor car and engaged Sidney Letzer, the delivery driver–mechanic, as his chauffeur. Leading landowners, businessmen and professionals followed the royal example, acquiring cars and chauffeurs to augment their horse transport facilities. The 6th Duke of Portland, for instance, purchased a large fleet of cars for use at Welbeck Abbey in Nottinghamshire and not only employed a head chauffeur and fifteen chauffeurs to drive and maintain them but also fifteen footmen to ride alongside the chauffeurs to open car doors and handle luggage, and two full-time washers to clean the cars. His contemporary, the 11th Duke of Bedford, retained a fleet of four cars and eight chauffeurs at his London home alone, in addition to those based at Woburn Abbey in Bedfordshire,

Footman standing alongside an early motor car outside a row of coach houses c1905.

his principal country residence. The London cars and chauffeurs were kept primarily for use around town and to transport members of his household and guests en route to Woburn Abbey as far as Hendon, where they changed cars and continued their journey in a car sent down from Woburn!

Landowners spent large sums of money in order to ensure that their motor cars were suitably housed and maintained in pristine condition. Coach houses were converted into garages or new garage blocks were built, usually with flats above to accommodate chauffeurs. Central heating was installed in garages to keep cars warm and dry and to facilitate easier starting, while inspection pits were dug underneath for maintenance purposes. Covered car washes were constructed to enable cars to be cleaned in all weathers. Petrol storage facilities were provided, often with a hand-cranked pump for fuelling vehicles more easily. On large estates, it was not unusual to have a fully equipped motor repair workshop complete with one or two dedicated mechanics – who might also be responsible for maintaining and servicing the electric lighting plant for the mansion.

Chauffeurs, like the motor cars they drove, were well treated by employers and rewarded accordingly. By the mid-Edwardian era they could command a weekly

Walter Wray, chauffeur to Dr Green at Killinghall near Harrogate, Yorkshire, c1910. The footman (standing on the far side of the car) not only opened the car door for the doctor and announced his arrival at a patient's house, but also opened gates across drives and roads.

wage of around £2-10/- (£2.50) to £3, at a time when a qualified gamekeeper or gardener earned £1 a week and an experienced farm labourer might be paid from 10/- (50p) to £1 per week depending upon the part of the country in which he worked. They were provided with a smart livery uniform consisting of a double-breasted tunic, peaked cap, breeches, leggings and boots, together with suitable protective clothing for use when servicing or cleaning cars. Chauffeurs, of course, benefited from the usual country estate perks of free housing and fuel, as well as generous tips from house guests.

Intrepid characters

Edwardian chauffeurs were intrepid characters, who frequently drove great distances over badly surfaced roads, many of which were little better than farm tracks, sharing the highway with horses and horse-drawn vehicles that were often difficult to pass or overtake. On dry summer days they became covered in road dust within minutes of starting out on a journey, while in inclement weather they could expect to get wet and mud-spattered. They often spent long hours on standby in the servants' hall at a distant country house or in the 'chauffeurs' room' at a hotel waiting to collect their employer and take him home. Upon their return they were expected to wash and polish the car before putting it in the garage, even if late at night or in the early hours of the morning!

The chauffeurs of the day were expected to drive to London prior to the start of the London season in early May, usually conveying important luggage or perishable produce, in order to provide transport facilities in town, while their employer and his household travelled to London in the comfort of a specially chartered train or set of reserved carriages from his local railway station. Similarly, they undertook the long and arduous journey north from London to the Scottish Highlands at the end of July or in early August so that a car would be available at their employer's shooting lodge for the duration of the sporting season, the employer and his party again travelling by train. In some instances a chauffeur might take a motor car to Scotland by sea, prior to making the onward journey to the lodge by road, as Geoffrey Braithwaite, whose father, Cecil, rented the Inverawe shootings and fishings in Argyllshire in 1910, recounts in his privately published autobiography, *Fine Feathers and Fish*:

> Instead of travelling by train to Inverawe, I went with Turner, our chauffeur, together with the Renault car, by boat from the General Steam Navigation Wharf on the Thames to Leith at Edinburgh and then by road to Inverawe. It took us three days and we had a most entertaining trip with a very convivial captain who kept us in fits of laughter with the many seafaring stories he told.

Shooting brakes and estate lorries

Many Edwardian chauffeurs not only drove motor cars for their employer, but also drove the purpose-built shooting brakes that were used to convey parties of Guns and their accoutrements on and off the shooting field during the autumn and winter months and drove the estate lorry, usually a cumbersome steam-powered vehicle, that was used to collect heavy goods from the local railway station. They often acted as loaders on shoot days, too, having been trained for the task by the head gamekeeper, or assisted the butler and footmen with shoot lunch preparations while on standby during the morning.

Advertisement for a Wolseley Station Car, 1905. Station cars were used to convey luggage from a railway station to a country house and to transport dogs and sporting equipment on the shooting field.

WOLSELEY SIDDELEY AUTO CARS.

Hold World's Record for Reliability.

"WOLSELEY" STATION CAR.

A new type of Car recently placed on the market to meet the demand for a vehicle equally suitable for the carriage of Luggage from Country Houses and for reaching Shooting Lodges at a distance. It is particularly adaptable for the latter purpose when a number of guns and dogs have to travel a long way. For this purpose the car body has been built extra wide and low. A 12 H.P. motor is fitted, and even the steepest hill can be easily surmounted with full load.

FULL PARTICULARS ON APPLICATION.

By Appointment to HER MAJESTY THE QUEEN.

THE WOLSELEY TOOL AND MOTOR CAR CO., Limited, YORK STREET, WESTMINSTER, LONDON, S.W.

The early days of motoring

The motor car was legalised for use on British roads in November 1896, removing the need for a red flag man to walk in front of a vehicle. Early motor cars were large, heavy and of robust construction and designed for use on unsurfaced roads, either of stone, gravel or hardened mud. Costing anything between £600 and £2,500 (between £40,000 and £150,000 at today's prices), they could often carry from two to ten people. On some country estates, a team of cart horses would be kept on standby whenever a car went out in case it broke down and had to be towed home or pulled out of a piece of soft ground. Car ownership in Great Britain increased from around fourteen or fifteen cars in 1895 to 1,000 in 1900, and 8,500 by 1905.

The outbreak of World War One

Following the outbreak of World War One, chauffeurs were head-hunted by the military authorities to drive and maintain motor vehicles, either on the home front or on the battlefields of Europe. Some enlisted in the Army Service Corps (renamed the Royal Army Service Corps in 1917) and were deployed as staff car drivers or lorry drivers, while others were recruited into the Royal Army Medical Corps as ambulance drivers. Chauffeurs with above average mechanical abilities invariably became mechanics in the Royal Engineers. Those with influential employers, however, usually ended up as officer's batmen, serving their master or one of his sons. In exceptional circumstances, a chauffeur of military age was exempted from joining the armed services if his employer was engaged on civilian work of national importance and was able to justify his need for a driver, but this was not common. Many chauffeurs chose not to return to private service after the cessation of hostilities in 1918, instead taking jobs as lorry drivers, taxi drivers, police

Having learned to drive a car prior to the outbreak of World War One, gamekeeper Ernest Grass was deployed as an Army staff car driver rather than as a front-line soldier for part of the conflict.

drivers or hotel car drivers, all of which offered higher pay and shorter working hours.

Chauffeurs really came into their own during the inter-war years from 1918 until 1939 when the motor car finally replaced horse-drawn vehicles as the principal mode of private road transport. Even the more traditional minor country landowners who had retained their traps and carriages for short journeys and used trains for long-distance travel had been obliged to switch over to the car because of the relatively high cost of maintaining a stables establishment and found it cheaper to employ a chauffeur rather than half a dozen or so men in the stables. The chauffeur was, indeed, an indispensable servant at this time as there were still relatively few owner–drivers around and those who could drive nevertheless enjoyed the prestige of being driven by someone else.

Multi-talented chauffeurs

Multi-talented chauffeurs were particularly sought after by the country landowners of the day, especially young men who were not imbued with the strict traditions of private service and were prepared to turn their hand to whatever task was demanded of them. Many doubled as chauffeur–valets and enjoyed a glamorous lifestyle

Chauffeur and ghillie on a Scottish estate c1925. In addition to driving long distances and maintaining cars in immaculate condition, the chauffeurs of the 1920s were often expected to undertake a wide range of other tasks.

accompanying their master on his travels and staying in stately homes or top hotels. It was not uncommon for such men to be sent to prestigious London shooting schools to learn how to handle a gun correctly in order that they could perform loading duties on the shooting field. Chauffeur–valets were frequently expected to act as caddies on the golf course or ghillies on the fishing river as and when required, too.

Life could be demanding for a chauffeur during the inter-war years, though. The chauffeur–valet to Brigadier Sir Joseph Laycock, for example, drove his employer from one shooting engagement to another overnight on a regular basis throughout the shooting season while his employer slept in the back of his Rolls-Royce and rose the following morning at the next destination in time to freshen up, eat breakfast and dress for the day's sport. His contemporary, George Gude, long distance chauffeur to the 2nd Duke of Westminster, was once requested by his employer to drive a car from the duke's Scottish shooting quarters at Lochmore in Sutherland to Naples in Italy in order to meet his private yacht the following week and enable one of his female guests to be driven from Naples to Mount Vesuvius for lunch. The mission accomplished, Gude was thanked by the duke and dispatched back to Lochmore. The duke, who spared no expense in the pursuit of pleasure, in the meantime returned to Scotland with his party by yacht!

World War Two and beyond

In 1939, when World War Two was declared, many chauffeurs of military age once again joined the armed forces for the duration, driving cars, lorries, ambulances or tanks, or became vehicle mechanics in the Army, the Royal Navy or the Royal Air Force. Some men, however, were exempted from military service and were deployed as civilian car or lorry drivers with government departments or were directed to work in factories producing equipment for the war effort. Elderly chauffeurs who were not called up generally combined driving duties, which were severely restricted due to petrol rationing, with household or general estate work and service in the Home Guard or one of the other home defence organisations.

Notwithstanding the fact that most landowners were now able to drive themselves, chauffeurs continued to be employed on country estates in the aftermath of the war, although some doubled as chauffeur–gardeners, chauffeur–butlers, chauffeur–handymen or chauffeur–estate workers and only drove on important occasions. By the 1960s they had become something of a rarity on all but the most prestigious of properties, being deemed to be an unnecessary and expensive luxury by the great majority of estate owners. Thereafter, chauffeurs became the sole preserve of royalty, senior members of the aristocracy, captains of industry, celebrities and others wealthy enough to afford them.

Tom Jones – chauffeur

Tom Jones was born in the Carmarthenshire hamlet of Felingwm in 1882. The eldest son of a carpenter and farmer, he did a variety of jobs before becoming a groom on the nearby Allterferin estate in the late 1890s. Shortly afterwards his employer, Edward Henry Bath, a wealthy Swansea copper merchant, smelter and ship owner, purchased a motor car and chose him as his chauffeur. Tom was subsequently sent to a Coventry car factory to learn to operate the vehicle before driving it back to Allterferin – it was the first car to arrive in Carmarthenshire. Sadly, the car was to be short lived, as Tom would recount

in later life. Constantly breaking down on the short journey to Carmarthen, it was regularly pulled home by a team of horses and proved to be something of an embarrassment to Mr Bath, who sold the vehicle and reverted to horse-drawn transport. Men and women ran into fields in fright when they saw the car coming, while horses bolted, which made the owner, a magistrate, and his chauffeur less than popular with the local residents!

In the circumstances, Tom had little choice but to work with horses once again. Having learned to drive a coach at Allterferin, he secured a job as personal coachman to Sir Charles Philipps, Bt. at Picton Castle in Pembrokeshire. His duties not only involved

Above: Perfectly turned out in a coachman's uniform, Tom Jones driving a pony and trap in front of Picton Castle, 1904.

Right: Part-time soldier: Tom Jones on horseback wearing the undress uniform of the Pembrokeshire Yeomanry Cavalry, 1904.

driving his employer on day-to-day business locally, but also travelling to London with the household for the 'season' aboard a specially chartered train from Haverfordwest to Paddington in order to assist the stables staff kept at the family's town residence. He served as a part-time soldier in the Pembroke Yeomanry Cavalry, too, which was commanded by his employer, was given two weeks' leave each year to attend the annual camp and was provided with a horse for the duration.

Tom continued to work with horses throughout the Edwardian era, either as a coachman, as a groom or as a hunt servant, although he did occasionally drive a car while employed as whipper-in to Mr Lloyd-Price's Harriers at Bryncothi in Carmarthenshire from 1908 until 1912. He finally decided to make a career in hunt service for good and moved from Wales to Farningham in Kent in 1912 after being appointed 1st whipper-in to the West Kent Harriers by the master, Captain Russell Johnson, a well-known hound breeder.

Tom Jones (on right) exercising Mr Lloyd-Price's Harriers c1909.

Several months after the outbreak of World War One, Tom was made redundant by Captain Russell-Johnson when the West Kent Harriers were disbanded after the captain's horses were taken by the Army Remount Department for use by soldiers. He tried to enlist in the Army but was told that he was over the age limit. Luckily, being able to drive a car, still a relatively

continued overleaf

uncommon skill, he found a job as chauffeur to the rector of Ulcombe, the Reverend Lord Theobald Butler, at Ulcombe near Maidstone in Kent, where he remained for around fourteen months.

Horses taken from landowners by the Army Re-Mount Department for use by soldiers on the battlefield and elsewhere.

Early in 1916, Tom returned to Wales to take a chauffeur's position with Robert Lougher Knight J.P., at Tythegston Court in Glamorganshire. He was paid £3 per week and provided with a rent-free house, fuel and other perks. His employer, a prominent country landowner, who served on numerous war-related committees was allowed to retain a chauffeur owing to the important nature of his work. However, Tom was called up by the Army in 1917 due to a shortage of drivers and had to appear in front of a military tribunal on three occasions before Mr Knight succeeded in getting him exempted from military service for the duration of the war. Tom continued to work at Tythegston until 1920.

Thereafter, Tom served as chauffeur to Dr Edward Roberts, a wealthy eye specialist, on the Pen-yr-Wern and the Aberllolwen estates near Aberystwyth in Cardiganshire from 1921 until 1931. He was on call twenty-four hours a day in case the doctor was summoned to an emergency at the local hospital and regularly drove his employer as far as Manchester or Cheltenham to visit private patients.

Tom subsequently became chauffeur to Captain T.P. Lewes, at Llanayron estate (now known as Llanerchaeron) in Cardiganshire, where he drove a white 1907 Rolls-Royce Silver Ghost, a grey 40-50 Sunbeam and a fawn AC

two-seater open tourer that was used for shopping trips and journeys around the estate. Before being allowed to drive the Rolls-Royce he had to undergo an 'on the job' assessment by a tutor sent from the Rolls-Royce factory in order to ensure that he could handle the vehicle correctly – the car was later sold to a local funeral director for £50 when the captain fell on hard times! In addition to driving the captain on local journeys and to hunting engagements during the season, he was responsible for the lighting supply system, powered by a water-driven dynamo with a back-up oil engine.

In the mid-1930s, Tom returned to Allterferin in his native Carmarthenshire to work as chauffeur for Captain William Daniel, whose family had purchased the property some years previously. He not only drove his master's cars, a motorised horsebox and the estate lorry, but also maintained the power plant that supplied electricity to the mansion. His employer, a wealthy colliery owner, spared no expense on motor cars, keeping his vehicles in a heated garage and changing them annually. Tom, himself, was well looked after, too. He lived in the bailiff's house on the home farm and was so well paid that he was able to buy his own car, an open-top Morris.

Captain Daniel re-joined his regiment following the outbreak of World War Two. Tom, now aged fifty-seven, was subsequently made redundant but was fortunate to secure a position as chauffeur to Lady Emily Butler, widow of Sir William Butler, chairman of Mitchells & Butlers Brewery, at Edgbaston in Birmingham. Being a countryman through and through he found it a little strange to live in the middle of a large city for the first

Above: Tom Jones with a Sunbeam motor car while in the service of Dr Roberts at Aberllolwen, 1928.

Below: Dressed in a modern chauffeur's uniform (breeches, leggings and boots had now been replaced by trousers and shoes), Tom Jones stands proudly beside a new Alvis saloon at Allterferin, 1937.

continued overleaf

Now a car owner himself, Tom Jones with his wife, Agnes, and daughter, Daisy, on the road in his open-top Morris near Allterferin, 1938.

time in his life. Nevertheless, he spent ten happy years working for Lady Butler, serving on a part-time basis in the Auxiliary Fire Service for much of the war. Lady Butler died in 1950, bequeathing him a legacy of £50. He then became chauffeur to Mr Grey, the proprietor of Grey's department store in Birmingham, at Beoley Hall in Worcestershire, where he remained until his retirement in 1952.

Tom Jones continued to drive until shortly before his death at the age of 89 in 1971, latterly in his daughter's Ford Anglia. He had an unblemished driving record, neither having had an accident nor a fine for a motoring offence in more than seventy years on the road.

Dunhill's
LIVERIES *for* AUTUMN & WINTER

Now is the time to consider the matter of your Chauffeur's Livery.
∴ Write for patterns and designs of latest productions. ∴

Best Triple Milled Melton
of unequalled quality, thoroughly proofed, and guaranteed to stand the hardest wear and still retain its smart appearance.

CUT AND TAILORED IN THE WEST END, NOT FACTORY MADE

THE "LANCER" WAIST OVERCOAT
No. 2822.—In Melton or Frieze. Brown, Green, Blue, Grey, Black and Claret. **3 Gns., 4 Gns. and 5 Gns.**
Jacket and Trousers to match, **3 Gns., 4 Gns. and 5 Gns.**

Complete Catalogues post free on request.

2, CONDUIT STREET, W.

88, Cross Street, MANCHESTER   72, St. Vincent Street, GLASGOW

Advertisement for Dunhill's chauffeurs' liveries, 1911.

8

THE BOATMAN

SOMETHING OF A rarity today other than on offshore island estates, the boatman was an important employee on all coastal and island properties during the nineteenth and the early twentieth centuries. His principal duty was to transport a landowner, his family and guests back and forth from the mainland by boat or to destinations more easily accessible by sea than land. He also collected essential supplies for the property and, in some instances, doubled as a sea fisherman and caught fish for the table in the 'big house'.

Coey, a small steam yacht of the type owned by a landowner with a coastal property during the Edwardian era and crewed by specially trained estate boatmen c1905.

Small coastal estates

Small coastal estates generally owned a fishing boat or sailing yacht of some description that was operated by the boatman with the assistance of staff from other departments who doubled as part-time crew members as and when required. Henry Miller, boatman to the Bond family at Tyneham in Dorset throughout the Edwardian era, however, combined his role with that of gamekeeper and not only took his employer on sea fishing trips in a boat crewed by footmen but also organised shoots, directing the Guns in a nautical manner with cries of 'fore' and 'aft', using compass points to direct them to their quarry. In appearance, Henry contrasted sharply with the well-groomed keepers of the day, dressed in his much-worn shapeless velveteens, their pockets bulging with furred and feathered game, his home-knit fishing gansey in thick navy blue, and his billycock hat, once black but long since changed to green by the salty winds.

Owners of large properties, either coastal or island, often possessed a small steam launch or steam yacht that was crewed by specially trained estate staff. The boatman in charge of such a vessel was invariably known as the 'captain' and was kitted out in appropriate maritime attire. He would be assisted by a fireman, who was responsible for coaling and running the engine, and one or two deckhands, all of whom would be issued with suitable seagoing clothing.

The SS *Puffin*, a typical estate steam launch belonging to Mrs Jessie Platt of Brocton Lodge, Stafford, and used to transport shooting guests to remote stalking beats at Eishken on the Isle of Lewis, her Scottish sporting property. The two boatmen who operated the launch can be seen standing second from left and on the far right. Courtesy of the Pairc Historical Society.

Charles Van Raalte, proprietor of Brownsea Island in Poole Harbour on the Dorset coast from 1901 until his death in 1908, employed a skipper, 'Captain' Tom Dean and a crew of three to run his 20-ton steam launch the *Blunderbuss*. The men were provided with expensive made to measure mariner's uniforms but were expected to start work at 5 a.m. in order to polish the brass fittings and to get up steam so the vessel could depart from Brownsea Quay at 8 a.m.!

Large private steam yachts

Some major landowners, of course, maintained large private steam yachts that were used for travelling abroad, cruising, racing or in connection with a Scottish sporting property during the shooting season. These, however, were operated on an independent basis and manned by professional sailors under the command of a sea captain rather than by estate employees. They were berthed at Cowes, South Shields or similar ports with suitable facilities during the winter months. The 4th Duke of Sutherland, for example, who owned a portfolio of country estates in England and Scotland, ran a 589-ton steam yacht *Catania*, built in 1895, for transport and pleasure purposes and employing a full ship's company. Unusually for a man of his social standing, he recouped a large proportion of the running costs by letting the vessel out on charter to wealthy clients when not required for personal use.

A large private steam yacht anchored off the Scottish coast c1910. Some major landowners maintained a fully crewed yacht for travelling abroad, cruising, racing or for use at a Scottish sporting property during the shooting season.

The boathouse at Didlington Hall, Norfolk, 1912. If an estate had a boating lake, it was usual for outdoor servants to act as boat handlers, maintain the boats in good condition and to assist with crewing duties if required.

9

THE LODGE KEEPER

SOMETIMES ALSO KNOWN as the gatekeeper, the lodge keeper was once a familiar figure on every country estate, large or small, living in a lodge at the entrance to one of the driveways that led from the public highway to the 'big house'. His (or her) principal role was to open the drive gates – made of wood or iron – to enable carriages, cars and pedestrians to enter the property, and to collect toll fees from favoured individuals who were authorised by the landowner to use particular driveways for business purposes. He was also responsible for maintaining the gates in pristine condition and lubricating the hinges, as well as for keeping out intruders.

The keeper of a main entrance lodge to a stately home was usually a full-time employee and was provided with a livery uniform to wear in order to ensure that he created a good impression whenever guests or tradesmen passed through the gates. He or a member of his family had to be available to open the gates twenty-four hours a day, seven days a week throughout the year whenever the sound of a coachman's whistle or the toot of a chauffeurs' horn was heard indicating that a carriage or a car was approaching. It was usual for those on foot or horseback wishing to enter an estate to knock the lodge door and ask to be let through the gates.

Opposite: The Archway at Fonthill Bishop, the main entrance lodge to the Fonthill estate in Wiltshire. Believed to have been designed by the architect, John Vardy, the lodge was built for Alderman William Beckford around 1756 and is still lived in today. *Courtesy of C.G. Hallam*

Left: Subsidiary entrance gate to one of the drives at Oakley Park, Shropshire, 1913. One lodge served as the living quarters for the lodge keeper and his family, while the other provided sleeping accommodation and primitive sanitary facilities. The notice on the gate states 'No Public Carriage Road. Keep Out. Oakley'.

Subsidiary lodges

Subsidiary lodges at the entrance to less well-traversed driveways tended to be manned either by estate pensioners or widows of servants, who lived on the premises on a 'grace and favour' basis and were paid a small wage, or by the wives of gamekeepers, woodmen and other outdoor staff members who undertook gate-opening duties as a condition of their husband's employment. For example, when the 3rd Lord Bolton engaged John Moore as an under-gamekeeper at Hackwood Park in Hampshire in 1877, he was told that he could live in London Lodge rent-free but that his wife would be required to 'attend to the gates and keep the gates, the driveway in the vicinity of the lodge and the lodge grounds in nice order'.

Housewife–lodge keeper posing for the camera with her family outside a gate lodge on an estate near Port Talbot in Glamorganshire.

Many gate lodges were designed by leading architects to fit in aesthetically in a landscaped country park environment and were either constructed in a similar style to the mansion on an estate or in the form of a folly. Others were simply 'model' cottages or small bungalows either side of a driveway, the lodge keeper and his family living in one and sleeping in the other. On the Lilleshall estate in Shropshire six of the twelve lodges, all built of brick and dressed stone during the first half of the nineteenth century in the 'model' style, contained a 'porch, entrance lobby, parlour, kitchen, scullery, larder, three bedrooms, coal house, tool store and pigsty, also either a water closet or earth closet'.

The gamekeeper's wife as a lodge keeper

There is no greater tax on the wife of a gamekeeper than when she has to attend to lodge gates. The occupants of a carriage will not often brook delay, and she has to be constantly on the watch for the rumble of wheels in the distance. Go away for a few moments she cannot, as if she did, a carriage would be certain to appear. Talk about the quick change artists seen on the London stage; it would be a revelation if they could see a gamekeeper's wife set about changing the workmanlike garments she wears in the morning for the more becoming apparel donned in the afternoon with a carriage rumbling in the distance towards the lodge gates. I do not wonder at the wife objecting to her husband taking a situation where the duty of attending to lodge gates falls to her lot. Besides a keeper's house should not be where the private and public roads join, as his movements are far too closely watched.

The Gamekeeper, July 1901

Ivy Lodge, Rendlesham, Suffolk – a 'folly' type gate lodge built by the 1st Baron Rendlesham during the early years of the nineteenth century.

Buck Gates Lodge, Thoresby Park, Nottinghamshire, c1900. Lived in by a succession of gamekeepers during the late nineteenth and early twentieth centuries, whose wives acted as lodge keepers, the gates were removed around 1940 and the property was abandoned at the end of World War Two, having served as a billet for a general and his wife during part of the conflict. The lodge was finally demolished in the late 1950s.

Extract from the sale particulars for the Lilleshall estate, the Shropshire seat of the 5th Duke of Sutherland, dated 1917, giving details of the gates adjacent to Newport Lodge situated at the main entrance to Lilleshall Hall:

> *The Newport entrance at the head of the principal carriage drive leading to the mansion is guarded by a set of magnificent wrought iron gates, the central pair having the Sutherland Monogram in gilded appliqué, the two supporting columns being about 18ft. high, on which are two lantern lights. Flanking these columns on each side is a grille en suite, connected with which on either side is a hand gate with 1895 in monogram, and each surrounded by a ducal coronet; these hand gates being supported further by two smaller grilles connected with large stone pillars with ball capitals.*

The demise of the lodge keeper

Following the outbreak of World War One, lodge keepers both young and old were redeployed on other more important duties and lodge gates were opened by coachmen, chauffeurs, horse riders and pedestrians as and when necessary, or were propped open permanently or removed entirely. In the aftermath of the war, lodge keepers were gradually dispensed with on most estates due to rising employment costs and lodges were either used to house staff or were rented out to members of the public. Some of the smaller lodges were simply abandoned and left to fall into disrepair, while subsidiary driveways on many properties were no longer maintained and became overgrown, being used only as farm or forestry tracks.

10

THE GARDENS

THE GARDENS SURROUNDING a country house were managed by the head gardener, not only for leisure purposes but to provide a constant supply of fresh vegetables, fruit, cut flowers and house plants for the household. Many gardens were originally laid out during the Tudor period but were completely redesigned and landscaped by professional landscape gardeners during the eighteenth century at a time when stately homes throughout Great Britain were being remodelled and upgraded. Landowners continued to lavish money on their gardens throughout

Formal gardens maintained in pristine condition at Holkham Hall, Norfolk, 1894.

Anticlockwise from below:
Flower borders and plant
houses at Tolmers Park,
Herfordshire, 1912.

Early lawnmower in use
outside a country house
c1905.

Gardeners on a country
estate posing for the
camera with an early
Ransomes lawnmower
c1905. Constructed largely
of cast iron, these machines
were heavy to operate
and were usually pushed
from behind by a gardener
and pulled from the front
by a boy using the rope
attached to the front of
the grass box.

the nineteenth and the early twentieth centuries, installing the latest state of the art
heated glasshouses and conservatories, and purchasing expensive imported plants.
Indeed, by the dawn of the Edwardian era in 1901, the gardens on a large, prestigious
estate could produce anything from asparagus and artichokes to apricots and peaches
in addition to the more common varieties of fruit and vegetables, along with a
remarkable variety of flowers, both outdoor and indoor.

Gardening activities everywhere were scaled down dramatically following the
outbreak of World War One, when large numbers gardeners of military age joined
the armed services in order to fight for their country. Gardens were subsequently
maintained by older men, pensioners and land girls, who grew less exotic varieties of
fruit and vegetables that were either used in country houses that had been converted
into hospitals or convalescent homes for soldiers and sailors or sold locally. After the
cessation of hostilities, the gardens at many large stately homes were revitalised, often
with emphasis on the flower gardens and pleasure grounds rather than on the kitchen
garden and the glasshouses. In contrast, those at smaller country houses owned by
impoverished members of the aristocracy and the landed gentry were either run
along modest lines by two or three gardeners or partially abandoned and looked
after by a gardener–handyman or a gardener–chauffeur on an 'as and when' basis
throughout the inter-war years. Since the end of World War Two many run-down
country house gardens have been restored and opened to the public by their owners,

or by the National Trust or similar organisations. The interest in preserving historic gardens has gone from strength to strength in recent years, creating employment for gardeners and ensuring the survival of traditional horticultural skills.

The flower gardens and pleasure grounds

The flower gardens and pleasure grounds were laid out specifically to a provide aesthetically pleasing views from a country house, as well as offering pleasant surroundings where a landowner could relax and entertain his guests, take walks and play croquet and other games. They generally consisted of formal and informal gardens planted to a particular theme, lawns, ornamental ponds and shrubberies, surrounded by a large area of enclosed parkland where deer and cattle roamed. The gardens would be maintained in pristine condition at all times, the gravel paths being raked, dead flowers being removed and statuary cleaned early in the morning every day before the household had risen. Likewise, the parkland, which was often interspersed with a number of monuments or follies where lunch or afternoon tea could be taken on a fine summer's day, was kept in good shape by members of the gardening staff and the estate yard team.

The kitchen garden

Unlike the flower gardens and the pleasure grounds, which were solely for leisure purposes, the kitchen garden was managed in order to provide fruit and vegetables for the household throughout the year. Situated either near the mansion or wherever the best soil could be found on an estate, the garden was usually surrounded by a brick or stone wall some 12 or 14ft high and divided into a number of separate compartments. The glasshouses, forcing houses and frames were invariably located within the kitchen garden complex, along with the boiler house, potting sheds, head gardener's house, unmarried gardeners' bothy (hostel), tool sheds and storage rooms for produce and gardening sundries.

On a large estate, the kitchen garden might cover several acres. The main kitchen garden at Lilleshall Hall in Shropshire, for example, extended to around 3 acres during the Edwardian era, with a 2¼ acre subsidiary kitchen garden adjoining, along with a 1 acre orchard stocked with apple and pear trees. The glasshouses within the gardens included a tomato house, two plant houses, a stove and greenhouse, three vineries containing a variety of grape vines and fig trees, a range of cucumber and melon pits (sunken greenhouses) and numerous cold frames. Unusually for the period, the bothy, which had six bedrooms, a mess room and other facilities, boasted a bathroom with a hot and cold water supply!

Advertising postcard issued to promote Carmona Plant Food depicting a collection of prize-winning vegetables grown in the kitchen garden at Welbeck Abbey, Nottinghamshire, exhibited by the 6th Duke of Portland at the Guaranteed Gardenalities Show in 1912.

1st Prize Group of . . CARMONA-FED VEGE-TABLES, Exhibited by His Grace The Duke of Portland, at the Guaranteed Gardenalities Show in August, 1912.

Experts expressed the opinion that the collection comprised some of the finest specimens seen for many years.

CARMONA PLANT FOOD can be obtained from your Seedsman.

Gardener standing beside a crop of outdoor tomatoes in a walled kitchen garden c1910.

Managed by a foreman and a dedicated staff of gardeners, a kitchen garden was expected to be able to produce a wide variety of vegetables, fruit and salad crops, both common and exotic, irrespective of the costs involved. Fresh produce was ordered from the garden daily by the mistress of the house or her cook whenever the family were in residence and delivered to the kitchens by a gardener. For instance, on the Rushmore estate on the Wiltshire–Dorset border, owned by the Pitt-Rivers family, the vegetables were gathered early in the morning, having been ordered the previous day, and taken to a special shed where they were trimmed and washed under a pump. They were then loaded on to a large wooden stretcher with two handles at each end and carried by two men from the kitchen garden to Rushmore Lodge, a distance of around ¾ mile. The men were met by the head gardener outside the lodge, who inspected the vegetables before they were taken into the kitchens and accepted by the cook. If Mr and Mrs Pitt-Rivers were staying in London for the season, a consignment of fruit, vegetables and flowers packed in large wicker hampers would be sent up by train from Tisbury station to Waterloo on a weekly basis and conveyed by pony and trap to their town house at 4 Grosvenor Gardens. Prior to the outbreak of World War One, it was not unusual for English landowners to have regular supplies of produce from their kitchen garden sent up to Scotland by rail throughout the sporting season.

Sadly, a large number of walled kitchen gardens were allowed to fall into decline in the aftermath of World War One due to staff shortages and rising maintenance costs. Some were abandoned in their entirety, others were taken over by professional market gardeners who paid a nominal rent in return for supplying the owner with vegetables and other produce as and when required. Many gardens continued to be operated along these lines or remained in a state of neglect until the late twentieth century when it became the fashion to restore walled gardens as tourist attractions, either returning them to their former glory or using them to grow flowers and produce for sale to members of the public.

Conservatories and house plants

The garden staff not only looked after the various outdoor gardens and glasshouses, but were also responsible for the heated conservatories attached to a country house, where palms, bananas, oranges and other exotic plants were grown, and for supplying cut flowers and house plants for the main rooms. Some landowners even employed a dedicated 'house gardener' whose sole task was to care for the house plants in the mansion, replenishing them as and when necessary. They made up buttonholes and sprays for the household to wear, provided floral decorations for the dinner table and other furnishings and undertook all other floristy work required by the mistress of the house or the housekeeper. Guidance for floral decorations could be obtained from

The conservatory at Dunraven Castle, Southerndown, Glamorganshire, c1920. Welsh seat of the Earls' of Dunraven, the property was demolished in 1962.

Floral Designs for the Table, a floristry manual for gardeners and others published in 1877 by John Perkins, head gardener to Lord Henniker at Thornham Hall in Suffolk, who specialised in such work.

The garden team at Wemyss Castle, Fife, 1905. Many Scottish landowners recruited trained gardeners from England rather than local men.

The garden team

The gardens on a country estate were managed by the head gardener, with the assistance of foremen gardeners, each of whom was in charge of a particular garden and had his own dedicated team of journeymen, under-gardeners, apprentices and garden boys. Large garden establishments usually employed more men than any other department on an estate and often took on part-time staff at busy times to carry out weeding, fruit picking and other tasks. For example, at Eaton Hall in Cheshire, the 2nd Duke of Westminster retained a head gardener and a permanent staff of forty-five gardeners of various grades during the Edwardian era to look after gardens that covered 100 acres, including a kitchen garden and 12 acres of glasshouses.

The Field 4 September 1858 wanted column

HEAD GARDENER – A married man, aged 34, with a thorough practical knowledge of the early forcing of fruit, flowers and vegetables. Can grow for exhibition if required. Good taste for the decoration of flower gardens and pleasure grounds. A first-class character from late employer.
Apply: "A.B." 5, Warwick Terrace, Warwick Road, Kensington

The head gardener

In charge of the gardens and pleasure grounds on a country estate, the head gardener was accountable to the land agent but usually reported to the landowner's wife on a daily or a weekly basis whenever she was in residence to discuss produce and flowers required for the mansion. He not only needed to be fully conversant with all branches of horticulture, but also had to be capable of supervising a large team of gardeners of all grades. Unlike other heads of department, who rarely kept records of any kind, he was expected to keep a diary or 'gardener's book' detailing daily work activities, planting, cropping, pruning and other information. The head gardener normally lived in a comfortable house within the walled garden complex, sometimes adjoining the bothy, which housed the unmarried gardeners, and was entitled to reasonable supplies of fruit and vegetables in addition to his wages and other perquisites.

Above: William Grass, head gardener to the shipping magnate, the 1st Viscount Furness, at Hamels Park, Hertfordshire with his infant son, Derrick (born in the head gardeners' house within the gardens) in 1928.

Right: Hamels Park, Hertfordshire, 1926.

The head gardener

The gardener, to understand his business well, and to be capable of undertaking management of a gentleman's garden and grounds, should not only be perfect in the ordinary business, and the regular routine of digging, cropping, and managing a kitchen garden, but should also be well versed in the nature of soils, manures, and composts, the best methods of propagating plants, shrubs, and trees, the management of the hothouse, greenhouse, conservatory, hotbeds; and the culture, not only of indigenous, but also of foreign and exotic productions.

The Complete Servant *by Samuel and Sarah Adams, 1825*

The foreman gardener

The foreman gardener was responsible for looking after one of the garden sections on an estate such as the kitchen garden, the flower gardens, the glasshouses or the pleasure grounds. Ranking immediately below the head gardener, he had his own staff of men to carry out the day-to-day work in his particular garden. Some major landowners with large garden establishments employed as many as half a dozen foremen in times past, all of whom were specialists in a given area, while on a small property one foreman sufficed, effectively acting as deputy-head gardener.

Memoirs of a foreman gardener

George Young, who served as a foreman gardener to the 6th Duke of Portland at Welbeck Abbey in Nottinghamshire from 1902 until 1908, provides a brief insight into his responsibilities as 'the Duchess's man':

> Soon after King Edward VII succeeded to the throne, I landed a job as a foreman to the head gardener at Welbeck Abbey, home of the Duke and Duchess of Portland. He told me that he would not be seeing much of me, as I would be 'the Duchess's man', in charge of three large conservatories, of an underground glass roofed corridor and of all the floral decorations in the Abbey. The conservatories, built in the style of the Crystal Palace, were about 20 ft. high and contained some very large camellias, palms, eucalyptuses and other exotics. Two or three men were required to carry them into the house. The corridor, about 16ft. wide and 100 yards long, contained groups of flowering plants, including specimen fuchsias and geraniums, which were renewed every two weeks from the glasshouses. It led directly from the picture gallery, which was 157 ft. by 64 ft and all underground, its flat roof being covered with shrubs; it was sometimes used as a ballroom. The corridor itself made a pleasant promenade, with seats among the flowers, soft lighting and fountains. From it an underground passage led to the Riding School over a distance of 1,070 yards.

The journeyman gardener

Upon completion of his apprenticeship or having risen from garden boy to under-gardener, a young man generally became a journeyman gardener on another estate in order to broaden his experience. Now qualified to work on his own without supervision, he often began to specialise in a particular branch of gardening such as maintaining flower gardens, vegetable production or greenhouse propagation. It was not uncommon for a journeyman to be employed in this capacity on a number of properties, perhaps for a term of one or two years at a time, before taking a foreman's position in the gardens at a large stately home, becoming a senior hand in the gardens at a medium-sized country house or a single-handed gardener to an upper middle-class household in a country town or the suburbs of a city. Traditionally, a journeyman was paid by the day or 'journée', although by the nineteenth century the great majority of landowners paid all gardening staff either quarterly, in arrears, fortnightly or weekly.

The under-gardener

The under-gardener on a country estate worked under the supervision of the head gardener or one of his foremen. He was either assigned to a particular garden on a more or less permanent basis or alternated between the different gardens as and when required. His duties usually included digging and trenching, hoeing, manuring, mowing, mixing potting compost, watering and other laborious tasks. After spending a couple of years as an under-gardener, a young man intent upon making a career in horticulture would progress to journeyman gardener or foreman gardener at a small establishment. Some under-gardeners, however, especially those who had taken up gardening later in life, were quite content to remain in the same garden for decades on end until they retired on a pension or became too old to work.

The apprentice gardener

Either a promising school leaver or a garden boy of above average ability, the apprentice gardener served an informal or an indentured apprenticeship for a set term of years. During this period he gained a good grounding in all branches of horticulture, working alongside experienced gardeners in the various gardens found on a country estate. On some of the more prestigious estates he was also expected to obtain an elementary knowledge of land surveying, botany and other relevant subjects by studying appropriate text books and manuals during his limited spare time. Generally speaking, only progressive landowners with large 'showpiece' gardens and professional nurserymen engaged apprentices.

The garden boy

Usually a school leaver keen to become a gardener, the garden boy started right at the bottom assisting the gardeners with their day-to-day duties as and when required and undertaking menial tasks such as weeding, raking paths, flower pot washing, cleaning tools and stoking the various boilers used to heat the frames and greenhouses. He either lived at home, if employed on a small local estate, or in the unmarried gardeners' bothy if working at a large establishment, where he might be expected to help out with the domestic arrangements in the absence of a full-time housekeeper. Having completed around two years' service in the gardens on a country estate to the satisfaction of the head gardener, a garden boy progressed directly to under-gardener or, alternatively, became an apprentice gardener.

Opposite: The under-gardeners at Newby Hall, Yorkshire, 1905. The author's great uncle, Arthur Hedley Grass (standing on the far right) later became a foreman gardener to the 9th Earl of Coventry at Croome Court in Worcestershire. All the men lived in the unmarried gardeners' bothy.

Life as a Garden Boy

Delmé Jones was employed as a garden boy in the gardens on the Llanayron estate in Cardiganshire for several years during the early 1930s. Interviewed in 2002, he recalls some details of his time at the property:

I started work as a garden boy for Captain T.P. Lewes at Llanayron in July 1931. The wages were 1/- (5p) a day and I had to keep myself. I had to work from 8 am to 6 pm. six days a week, or from 8 am until dark in winter. The garden staff consisted of the head gardener, Mr Maskell, the under-gardener, Rees Williams and John 'Cwmbach' who helped in the gardens and looked after the poultry on the home farm.

The walled gardens were only half kept at this time. The greenhouses were looked after fairly well. There was a fan-trained nectarine in one. Tomatoes were grown in another. There were two vineries producing black and white grapes and there was a greenhouse where pot plants were grown for the house. The greenhouses were heated by a boiler and a system of hot water pipes, fired by wood from the estate and surplus small coal or slack which had accumulated in the coal house near the billiard room. Whenever more wood was required for the boiler, the captain and Mr Maskell selected a suitable tree from the plantation near Llanayron mansion. It would be felled by Rees Williams and John 'Cwmbach', using a cross cut saw. Afterwards the trunk was cut into six foot lengths which were again split by sledge hammer and wedges into about six pieces and then carted to the sawmill and sawn into two foot lengths which were then carted to the potting shed and stacked handy to the boiler.

Delmè Jones (seated on right in front row) with members of his family in the walled gardens at Llanayron, 1933.

Captain Lewes was very particular about keeping the surroundings of the house tidy. The gravel driveway and paths had to be weeded regularly and the white entrance gates had to be washed daily to keep them clean. Every Saturday afternoon at 3 pm. the gravel around the house had to be raked with a large wooden rake to get rid of wheel marks etc. We could not start before 3 pm. as Mrs Lewes was terminally ill at this time and was resting until that hour.

Work in the gardens went on in a leisurely way, no great rush to do anything. Occasionally the Captain 'blew up' but things were soon back to normal.

The roadman or labourer

Found on a large country estate with an extensive network of carriage driveways, the roadman or labourer was responsible for keeping a particular driveway or a section of it in pristine condition, raking the gravel, removing weeds, cleaning the drains, carrying out minor repairs and clearing fallen leaves during autumn and winter. On some properties, he also helped to maintain the surfaced forestry roads which were used for timber extraction and shooting purposes, as well as the gravel paths in the gardens and through the parkland. In the region of between forty and fifty roadmen were employed by the 6th Duke of Portland at Welbeck Abbey in Nottinghamshire during the Edwardian era, in addition to around sixty gardeners of various grades!

List of garden staff employed by the 8th Duke of Beaufort at Badminton Park, Gloucestershire in 1836:

1 head gardener
1 second gardener
1 florist
12 men in kitchen garden
5 women in kitchen garden
6 men in flower gardens and pleasure grounds
3 women in flower gardens and pleasure grounds
2 men in nursery (fruit trees, evergreens, etc.)
1 woman in nursery

Total number of men and women: **32**

Inspecting beehives c1910. Bees were kept on the home farm on many country estates to provide honey for the mansion. The bees were usually looked after by a farm worker, who received honey as part of his remuneration package in return for his services.

11

THE HOME FARM

ONE OF THE most important departments on every country estate until the inter-war years, when in-house farming operations were scaled down or disbanded entirely on many properties, the home farm produced meat and dairy products for use in the mansion. Usually laid out along 'model' lines, with farm buildings that were designed to be beautiful as well as utilitarian, which enabled a landowner and his guests to inspect the livestock without getting too dirty, the farm also doubled as a 'demonstration farm', rearing exhibition quality sheep, cattle pigs, shire horses and poultry, and promoting good husbandry among the tenant farmers and smallholders. Managed by the bailiff (farm foreman) the farm might employ twenty or thirty men and maids, ranging from stockmen, shepherds, dairymaids, carters and other skilled specialists to general agricultural labourers, itinerant hedgelayers and seasonally recruited harvest workers from Scotland or Ireland.

Hedgelayers taking a breather beside a section of newly laid hedge c1950. Hedgelaying on a home farm was either carried out by itinerant hedgers who charged by the chain (20.1168m), or undertaken by farm workers during slack periods.

In *The Book of the Landed Estate* published in 1869, Robert Brown, land agent to Major Henry Stapylton on the Wass Estate in Yorkshire, gives a brief definition of the home farm on an estate, followed by some sound advice on running such an establishment efficiently:

> *The term 'Home Farm' is applied to the farms which landed proprietors keep under their own management. They are usually kept in-hand for the purpose of affording a pastime and amusement to the landlord and his family, and also for the purpose of supplying the numerous articles of farm produce required by a large establishment, and occasionally with the view of showing an example in farming to the tenants on the estate.*
>
> > *The chief objects to attend to in carrying out a home farm are the following:-*
>
> *The employment of a skilled, sharp, shrewd, and active farm bailiff, who is thoroughly honest.*
>
> *All the farm servants should be thoroughly honest, and zealously faithful in the discharge of their duties.*
>
> *When if practicable to do so, it would tend to a good result if both farm bailiff and labourers had an interest in the farm; that is to say, if they were allowed a certain wage and a percentage besides on the profits.*
>
> *The proprietor should take an active supervision himself; if this cannot be done, his agent should do so; but avoiding at the same time, unnecessary interference with the arrangements of the bailiff, and no step should be taken without consulting him.*
>
> *If any experiments are tried, they should be done at the expense of the farm.*
>
> *Every article, however small, that is supplied by the farm to the proprietor's establishment, and also any cartage to any other department of the estate, should be regularly charged for, and each department debited with the amount. Accounts for such articles and other claims should be sent by the farm bailiff monthly to the person in charge of each department.*

Farm labourers sharpening their scythes while hay making in the traditional manner, 1900.

The bailiff

The man in charge of the home farm on a country estate, the bailiff was effectively the farm manager, farming the land and supervising the staff, sometimes with little or no input from his employer. He might also be responsible for buying and selling livestock and exhibiting cattle, horses and other animals at shows. His salary varied according to the size of the farm, although he was generally provided with a substantial house within the precincts of the farmyard and a pony and trap or a horse for transport, along with free fuel, milk, butter, meat and other produce. On some estates he was allowed to augment his income by taking in a pupil (often the younger son of a landed gentleman or urban businessman) and teaching him the rudiments of farming in order that he could set up a farm on his own account, either in Great Britain or the colonies.

The carter

Undoubtedly the highest-ranking employee on the home farm after the bailiff, the carter provided the 'horsepower' for ploughing and harrowing, mowing and reaping, carting crops from field to barn or stackyard, conveying produce to market, collecting supplies from the nearest town or railway station, and numerous other farming

Clockwise from above:
Carters with a prize-
winning team of Suffolk
Punches belonging
to Kenneth Clarke of
Sudbourne Hall, Orford,
Suffolk, 1909.

Carter with a dung cart
c1910.

Ploughman on a Suffolk
estate, 1919.

operations that utilised horse-drawn machinery. Known also as the waggoner, the horseman, the horsekeeper or the teamsman in certain parts of the country, he not only handled the cart or shire horses in the field but also prepared them for the day's work, fed and watered them throughout the day, cleaned them and returned them to their stalls at night and generally looked after their welfare. He was in charge of the stables on the farm, maintained the harness equipment in good order and took horses to the farrier whenever they needed to be reshod. On a large home farm the horses came under the control of a head carter who might have half a dozen or more carters working beneath him, as well as a man trained in farriery who operated a small forge adjacent to the stables for shoeing purposes.

The ploughman

The ploughman ploughed the fields on the home farm as and when required using a plough drawn by horses or oxen prior to the introduction of steam- and tractor-powered ploughs. Usually a farm labourer or a carter assigned to ploughing duties by the bailiff, he was a highly skilled individual capable of ploughing to a set pattern, working a wooden or a metal plough and managing horses.

The stockman

Responsible for the herd of beef cattle kept to provide meat for the mansion, the stockman also handled the bulls, bred beef and dairy cattle for the home farm and produced bullocks. He might also be in charge of the teams of oxen (castrated male cattle used as draught animals), if an estate used oxen for ploughing and carting purposes. In addition to his wages, he was provided with free accommodation, milk and other perquisites.

Right: Stockman (on left) with a trio of well turned out bullocks c1910. Judging by their dress, the gentleman in the centre is his employer and the man on the right, the farm bailiff.

Below: Oxen ploughing on an Essex estate c1910.

The cowman

The cowman or dairyman looked after the herd of dairy cattle on the home farm, milked the cows, dealt with calving operations and, on some country estates, made cheeses for the mansion. His principal duties involved taking the cows back and forth from the pastures or the cow yard to the milking parlour, keeping the parlour spotlessly clean and maintaining the cowsheds in good order. In common with other skilled farm workers, he was paid slightly more than a labourer, given a tied cottage and supplied with a daily allowance of milk.

The dairymaid

Either an outdoor or an indoor servant, depending upon the establishment where she was employed, the dairymaid dealt with the milk and cream produced by the estate cows (the cows were normally milked by the cowman or the dairyman), churned butter for use in the mansion, made cheese, looked after poultry and collected the eggs. She normally lived-in at the home

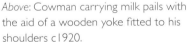

Above: Cowman carrying milk pails with the aid of a wooden yoke fitted to his shoulders c1920.

Left: The dairy at Welbeck Abbey, Nottinghamshire, 1910. Some large estates had a 'model' dairy such as the one depicted here that not only enabled the dairymaids to produce their wares in superlative working conditions, but also allowed the landowner and his guests to inspect operations without risk of soiling their clothes and footwear.

farm and was a member of the farm staff if the estate had a large dairy, but might come under control of the cook and live in the servants' quarters if the dairy was small and situated adjacent to the kitchens.

An extract from the sale particulars for the Lilleshall estate, the Shropshire seat of the 5ᵗʰ Duke of Sutherland, dated 1917, giving details of the dairy buildings that, unusually, included on-site accommodation for the dairymaid:

THE DAIRY BUILDINGS – built of stone and tiled – Octagon-shaped dairy, with porcelain tiled walls and floors, and dairymaid's accommodation, consisting of two living rooms, scullery, larder, w.c. and coal house, three bedrooms and cheese room.

The poultryman or maid

Known also as the poultry keeper, the poultry man or maid managed the flocks of chickens, ducks, turkeys and geese on a large home farm where the dairymaid was solely engaged in processing milk, churning butter and other dairy work. He or she collected eggs for culinary purposes and killed and plucked birds for the table as and when required. Often a young, unmarried person, the poultry man or maid usually lived-in at the home farm.

Poultryman and his family feeding turkeys c1910.

The shepherd

The shepherd was responsible for managing the flock of sheep on the home farm, which provided lamb and mutton for the mansion and wool for the manufacture of clothing. His duties entailed folding (moving and setting up hurdles in a field in which the sheep were being fed) the flock on a daily basis, lambing the sheep during early springtime and assisting in the annual sheep shearing operations, which generally took place in June. He earned slightly more than a farm labourer and was paid a 'lambing bonus' of around 6d (2½p) for every lamb that he reared. Single shepherds invariably lived in a mobile 'shepherd's hut' located in the vicinity of their flock, which could be moved around by a carthorse as and when necessary. Married men were provided with a tied cottage, but were expected to live on site in a hut during the lambing season in order to carry out their work effectively.

Above: Shepherd on the Sussex Downs, 1936.

Left: Shepherd moving a flock of sheep on a country estate c1910.

113

Above left: Pigman attending to his herd c1920.

Above right: A Hampshire farm labourer and his wife outside their cottage, 1890.

The pigman

Employed to look after the herd of pigs that were kept to provide pork and bacon for the mansion, the pigman was a semi-skilled agricultural worker and lived in a tied cottage on the home farm. He liaised with the local pig killer whenever a pig needed killing, making the necessary preparations beforehand. On many estates, he undertook other agricultural duties as and when necessary.

The farm labourer

Sometimes referred to as an agricultural labourer or a general farm worker, the old-fashioned farm labourer was in fact a multi-talented individual who could turn his hand to a wide variety of tasks. His work on the home farm might include ploughing, haymaking and harvesting, rick building and thatching, draining, hedging and ditching, and handling livestock and poultry, as well as acting as a beater on a shoot day and assisting the gardeners or the foresters whenever extra help was needed. He was either hired annually or employed permanently depending upon the policy of the landowner, provided with a fairly basic tied cottage and generally paid according to the labourers' rates prevalent in the district where he worked.

Above: Farm labourers building a rick by hand in the time-honoured manner …

Left: …and with the aid of an early mechanical elevator powered by an oil engine. Both photographs c1900.

Below: Neatly thatched ricks on a Northumberland farm c1910.

Details of the home farm buildings at East Farm, Fovant, Wiltshire, a 610 acre farm, as listed in the sales prospectus for the Fovant estate, 1919:

THE HOME FARM BUILDINGS
Well arranged, of modern design, and substantially built of Stone and Slate, comprise:-

NORTH RANGE – Coal-house, Engine-house, Root-house, Manure-house, Waggon Shed (with 4 bays) with Granary over all, Tool-house, Open Shed (2 bays) with Yard in Front.

WEST RANGE – 2 cow-houses for 3 cows in each with Feeding Gangways. Nag Stables, containing Loose-box, 3-stall Stable, Harness Room, Chaise-house, Cart Horse Stable for 8 horses, detached range of Piggeries.

EAST RANGE – Cooling-house with paved floor, enclosed Shed and Dressing Barn with paved floor and Loft over all.

THE CENTRE is enclosed by a large covered Yard, which is fitted with Cow-stalls to tie 51 cows, with paved floors, Channels, Mangers and Feeding Gangways with Fodder Gallery on 3 sides.

WATER SUPPLY – There is an excellent water supply obtained from a deep well in Engine-house on North of the Buildings with a Tangye's Deep Well Pump and 2½ hp Oil Engine complete, the water being distributed to the House, Farm Buildings and Cottages.

Farm workers celebrating the 'harvest home' with a barrel of Bass XXX c1910.

12

THE FORESTRY DEPARTMENT

FROM THE EARLY nineteenth century until the end of the Edwardian era, virtually every country estate, either large or small, maintained a forestry department in order to produce home-grown timber for building work, for fencing and gate making, and for use in the gardens and on the home farm. Managed by the head forester, with the assistance of under-foresters, woodmen and labourers, the department worked in close cooperation with the head gamekeeper and the hunt establishment to ensure that essential forestry activities did not conflict with shooting and hunting interests. On prestigious properties that were operated primarily for shooting, it was not uncommon for the head gamekeeper to act as head forester for this reason.

Well-managed traditional forestry plantations on the Bentley Manor estate in Worcestershire. The clump of trees in the centre of the photograph is a hunting covert, planted to harbour foxes.

The enthusiasm for estate forestry

An interest in forestry first began during the second half of the eighteenth century when the wealthier members of the aristocracy and the landed gentry started to landscape and develop country estates for aesthetic and sporting purposes. Large blocks of woodland, clumps, avenues, shelter belts, park trees and other features were planted by labourers and others in selected locations, chosen by a professional landscape gardener such as Capability Brown or Humphrey Repton, who often carried out all the improvement works on a contract basis. Thereafter, the newly planted trees were generally maintained by the estate labourers under the supervision of the landowner, himself, or his land agent.

Progressive landowners, realising that woodlands needed to be managed in a proper manner rather than left in the hands of inexperienced labourers, started to recruit professional foresters from Scotland during the early years of the nineteenth century. These men, who were relatively well educated, not only established some of the first forestry departments on English estates and recruited and trained under-foresters and woodmen, but were also responsible for the introduction of commercial conifer plantations on impoverished land. Scottish foresters had become highly sought after by the late Georgian era, both for their efficient working practices and

Woodmen on a country estate standing beside a newly felled tree c1905. The cross-cut saw leaning against the tree trunk on the left of the photograph was used for felling prior to the introduction of the chainsaw.

for their financial acumen. Indeed, by the early Victorian period, according to A.C. Forbes, writing in English Estate Forestry in 1906: 'It was as much the correct thing for an estate to have a Scotch forester as it was for a nobleman's establishment to have a French chef.'

Estate forestry was undoubtedly at its peak between 1850 and 1914. Mature trees planted during the second half of the eighteenth century were harvested and converted into timber for building purposes or furniture making. Historic working coppices were actively managed to produce green wood products. Large

Members of the Canadian Forestry Corps felling a tree on a Devon estate, 1916.

areas of woodland were replanted with deciduous trees. New woodlands were laid out, with game preservation in mind. Hunting coverts were planted in parks and on farmland for the purpose of harbouring foxes. Foresters and woodmen were employed in large numbers on estates throughout the country in order to carry out all of these tasks.

The effects of World War One

The outbreak of World War One had a catastrophic effect on estate forestry. Foresters and woodmen joined the armed forces to fight for their country on the battlefields of Europe or the high seas, leaving woodlands to fall into neglect. Large areas of mature woodland were subsequently felled by members of the Canadian Forestry Corps, assisted by Portuguese labourers, in order to make up the shortfall in imported timber required for pit props, railway sleepers and construction purposes, leaving forests everywhere in a state of dereliction.

In the aftermath of the war, only the wealthier landowners had the financial or staff resources available to revitalise their woodlands. Those that did often planted conifers rather than deciduous trees, encouraged by the Forestry Commission (formed in 1919 to expand Britain's forests and woodlands), or even sold or leased their derelict woodlands to the commission. In many instances, woods and forests were now looked after on a part-time basis by a gamekeeper–woodman or a farm worker–woodman rather than by a dedicated forestry team.

The Forestry Commission

Since this time, the Forestry Commission has become a key player in the forestry industry, dictating national forestry policy, managing numerous state-owned forests and regulating operations in woodlands on private country estates. Committed landowners with an interest in forestry have, however, continued to manage estate woodlands, either on an in-house basis with their own staff or by using specialist contractors, and over the past fifty years or so have played a lead role in replanting woods with deciduous trees rather than conifers.

Robert Brown, land agent to Major Henry Stapylton on the Wass Estate in Yorkshire, outlines some of the qualities needed for a man to become a head forester in *The Book of the Landed Estate* published in 1869:

> *Anyone desirous of following out the profession of a forester should receive an efficient and careful training, as much as a farm bailiff or gardener. It is very necessary, indeed, that anyone trusted with the management of extensive and valuable woodlands should be properly educated for his trust, and that he should be active and conscientious in everything he does.*
>
> *He should have received a good education in the common branches usually taught in our schools. He should be able to measure land, so that he may take correct plans of plantations and their acreage. He should have a fair knowledge of botany, so that he may be able to describe trees when required. He should also know the different qualities of soils, so that he will know what soil suits one kind of tree and what another.*
>
> *Besides the theoretical knowledge stated, it is still more necessary that a forester should be trained in the woods of some landed proprietor where there is a thoroughly good forester.*

The head forester

The man in charge of the forestry department on a large country estate, the head forester was directly accountable to the land agent who managed the property. His responsibilities traditionally included tree planting and maintenance, harvesting and converting timber for in-house building purposes or for sale, running a tree nursery looking after areas of coppice woodland, as well as maintaining woodland rides and coverts for game preservation or fox hunting. He was assisted in his work by a team of foresters, general woodmen and labourers, and was also in charge of supervising any coppice workers, tree fellers, chair bodgers or other itinerant craftsmen who might be working in the woodlands.

The under-forester

Employed to assist the head forester on a country estate with extensive areas of woodland, the under-forester might also act as foreman over the woodmen and the forestry labourers. In times past, it was not uncommon for several under-foresters to work on a large property, each man having responsibility for a particular section and his own squad of men.

The woodman

Something of a jack of all trades, the estate woodman carried out various day-to-day forestry tasks ranging from tree planting and timber felling to hedge and fence maintenance and ditch clearance. On some properties he was expected to undertake

Gamekeepers and woodmen posing for the camera beside a newly felled and dismembered tree c1910.

rabbit clearance in the woodlands, to act as a beater on shoot days and to keep a watching brief for any signs of poaching activities. He usually worked in conjunction with other woodmen, but on a small or a sparsely wooded estate could be employed on a single-handed basis.

The woodman, like the gamekeeper, traditionally lived rent-free in a tied cottage or lodge on his patch. His perks generally included an annual allowance of firewood and the right to collect fallen tree branches, trimmings and old tree roots for additional fuel, along with the occasional brace of rabbits whenever there was a big shoot on an estate.

The woodward

Found on country estates in some areas as a general woodman or a woodman–gamekeeper until the mid-nineteenth century, the post of woodward became obsolete after land owners started to employ forestry staff and gamekeepers on extensive scale The occupation of woodward dates back to the Medieval period, when it was customary for a lord of the manor to appoint a man to look after the manorial woodlands at the annual manor court. The title is still used today on a ceremonial basis in certain court leets.

Oxen hauling timber poles on a Sussex estate c1910.

PRIZE SUSSEX OXEN

13

ITINERANT CRAFTSMEN

IN ADDITION TO maintaining a large staff of professional tradesmen and semi-skilled workers in order to ensure that a country estate was run in a smooth and self-sufficient manner, most landowners hired itinerant craftsmen on a temporary or a seasonal basis to undertake specific tasks. Gangs of men from Ireland and Scotland were taken on to assist with haymaking and harvest operations; threshing tackle and ploughing contractors, who brought along their own steam-powered machinery, were employed in some areas; woodmen of varying kinds were hired to help with hedging and ditching, coppicing, fencing and other jobs; trappers were contracted to clear rabbits and moles; Fruit and hop pickers were engaged on properties that produced such commodities; craftsmen proficient in less common disciplines were taken on, too, often according to the geographical location of an estate. Either paid for their work in cash or allowed to take and sell woodland and other products in return

Fruit pickers on a Kent estate c1905. Itinerant farm workers, local housewives and gipsies were recruited on a temporary basis during harvest time to gather and pack apples, pears, cherries, strawberries and other varieties of commercially grown fruit.

for manufacturing and supplying a landowner with his annual requirements, these men usually lodged with an estate employee, a tenant farmer or simply lived rough in a makeshift tent in the woods or fields.

The coppice worker

The coppice worker harvested the underwood growing from coppice stools (stumps) in blocks of coppice woodland between the months of November and March. Usually a self-employed villager who did general farm work at other times of the year, he either

purchased the standing underwood by the block (sometimes also known as a 'cant', a 'coupe' or a 'lug') at a woodland auction held in early autumn or paid a set fee to a landowner in return for the right to cut a number of blocks, often providing any coppice products required by an estate in part payment. Blocks were cut on a five- to a sixteen-year cycle, depending upon the size of wood required and the type of tree species. After cutting season had finished, the coppice worker usually stayed on site until May or June in order to produce hurdles, fencing rails, poles for hop growing, thatching spars, pea and bean sticks, besoms, tent pegs, pheasant catchers and other coppice products, which he sold to local people, market traders or commercial buyers from urban areas. He used the leftover wood to make brushwood faggots for firing cottage ovens and disposed of any remaining waste as kindling for lighting fires.

Top: Coppice worker carrying a bundle of newly cut pea sticks c1910.

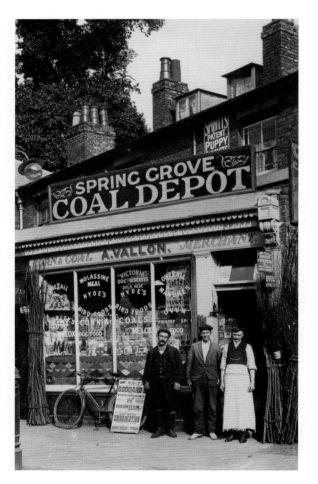

Left: Coppice products on display outside the Spring Grove Coal Depot at Isleworth, Middlesex, 1910. Note the bean sticks on the far left of the photograph and the besom (birch twig broom) on the far right. Such products found a ready market among gardeners and allotment holders in towns and cities.

The pig killer

Once a familiar figure in the countryside in the days when most cottagers kept a pig or two in order to supply meat for the household, the pig killer not only slaughtered and butchered pigs for ordinary folk but also provided his services to estate home farms and tenant farmers as and when required. Usually an itinerant butcher or a villager who had picked up pig-killing skills from a friend or a relative, he was either paid in cash or kind and often took the haseletts (prime joints of lean pork cut near the backbone of the pig) in part payment for his work. In many villages pig killing took place on a specific Saturday morning that coincided with 'a rising moon' when, according to rural tradition 'flitches would take salt properly'. Killing would be carried out on a specially made 'pig form', an essential piece of equipment owned by cottager and country landowner alike, on which the pig was subsequently cut up and the flitches salted.

Pig killer (on left wearing butcher's apron and holding knife in right hand) standing beside a newly slaughtered pig c1910. The straw placed on and around the carcase would be ignited in order to burn off the body hair.

The charcoal burner

Found predominantly on estates in the heavily wooded areas of southern England, the charcoal burner paid the landowner a small rental fee in return for being allowed to cut cordwood from which he produced charcoal using a home-made kiln constructed of straw turfs, earth, leaves and logs, a process that took around a week. He lived in a tent or rough wooden hut on site throughout the charcoal burning season – which ran from about August to November – in order that he could attend to the kiln fires every few hours. Having successfully completed the charcoal 'burn' and allowed things to cool down, he harvested the resultant charcoal, broke it into small lumps and packed it into sacks ready for sale for fuel, for use in the chemical industry or as an ingredient in the manufacture of ferrous metals.

The mole catcher

In times past the mole catcher performed a valuable service within the rural community, clearing moles, rats and other small vermin from country estates, farms and gardens. Often these men were retired gamekeepers, too old to carry out keepering duties, but who wanted to keep active and to earn some extra money to supplement their pension.

Mole catching, as a profession, appears to date back to the mid-eighteenth century, when churchwardens and parish overseers offered 'bounty payments' for the destruction of moles, rats, foxes, polecats and other predatory creatures. The early mole catchers usually worked on a self-employed basis, being paid an annual retainer by landowners and farmers, as well as receiving a fee for each 'tail' accounted for.

Mole catcher c1910.

Eighteenth and early nineteenth century estate accounts rarely mention individual 'tail' payments made to mole catchers, but often list a monthly vermin payment. For example, in October 1812, Lord Rivers, owner of the Rushmore estate in Wiltshire, paid a Mr Longman £1-0/-6d (£1.2½p), for 'Killing moles and other vermin'. Surviving records kept by the Marquess of Bristol at Ickworth in Suffolk in 1849 note that 2d (1p) a 'tail' was paid for moles, the same rate as for rats, both of which compared favourably with 'old sparrows' at ½d a 'head'. The annual retaining fee paid to the local mole catcher by the Earl of Leicester at Holkham Hall in Norfolk at this time amounted to £1-1/- (£1.05).

From the mid-nineteenth century until the outbreak of World War One, many large sporting estates employed a full-time mole catcher, who either worked for the game department or on the garden staff. Landowners found that this system worked better than hiring a casual man, who might turn up sporadically and help himself to the odd rabbit, pheasant or partridge 'for the pot' while carrying out his duties!

Mole catchers and gamekeepers prospered during this period, earning sizeable amounts of money from the sale of moleskins to the manufacturers of moleskin waistcoats and ladies coats. In 1901, a single skin could be sold for as much as 4d or 5d (2p). Prices later increased to more than 1/- (5p) with the advent of the motor car, as moleskin motor capes became fashionable and each one took from around 700 to 1,200 skins to complete.

Vermin accounts kept during the early twentieth century occasionally list annual mole 'bags', providing some idea of mole population levels at this time. For example, on the 25,000 acre Elveden estate in Suffolk, a total of 3,629 moles were killed in 1911, and 2,064 in 1912. In comparison, 6,779 rats were taken on the property in 1911, and 5,395 in 1912.

Unlike many other estate activities, mole catching continued throughout World War One, mainly because most of the men involved were above military age and were capable of acting as general vermin killers, while gamekeepers were away in the Army or the Navy. Moleskins were much in demand for the production of specialist military clothing during this period and mole catchers enjoyed a bonanza, selling skins for as much as 2/- (10p) each.

Following the end of the war, landowners were forced to make economies due to punitive taxation imposed by the government. Virtually every mole catcher was then made redundant. The job was subsequently carried out by a gamekeeper, on a casual basis by the village odd job man or by a farm worker in his spare time.

During the 1920s, '30s and '40s, freelance mole catchers either charged farmers and landowners around 6d (2½p) per acre per annum for clearing moles from their fields or were paid by the 'tail'. They then cured and sold the skins to furriers or skin and feather merchants such as Horace Friend & Co. of Wisbech, earning around 3d (1½p) to 6d (2½p) a skin, depending upon the quality. The skins were usually dispatched by post or rail to the buyer, and were often returned without payment if the demand was low!

From the 1940s onwards, an increase in the use of poisons and rodenticides to kill moles, some of which needed to be administered by a specialist pest control officer, led to a decline in the number of mole catchers working in the countryside. A few, mainly elderly, men remained in the profession until the early 1980s, principally to earn 'beer money' from the sale of skins, but ultimately gave up when skins became almost worthless due to a drop in demand. In recent years, however, men (and a number women) have started to take up mole catching as a full-time occupation once again, eradicating moles from gardens in rural and urban areas rather than clearing them from agricultural land.

The cider maker

The travelling cider maker was an annual visitor on estates in parts of the West Country, the Welsh border counties, Hampshire, Yorkshire and other districts where cider rather than beer was the local drink for farm hands, rural craftsmen and other manual workers. Using either a mobile press or a static press in the estate yard or

Travelling cider maker at work near Ringwood in the New Forest, Hampshire, c1925.

elsewhere, he produced cider from apples grown on the property, a process that involved pressing the apples to extract the juice, and pouring the juice together with a suitable quantity of water into barrels for fermentation. The resultant cider was then transferred to earthenware jars for storage upon completion of fermentation and distributed to eligible outdoor staff at mealtimes, either by the farm bailiff or the butler. Cider was rarely if ever issued to household servants in the mansion, for obvious reasons!

The rabbit trapper

Engaged to clear rabbits from farm land on country estates in areas with a high rabbit population, the trapper worked primarily during the autumn and winter months, using gin traps, snares, ferrets and nets to catch his quarry. He either leased the trapping rights over a certain acreage on a seasonal basis from a landowner for an agreed sum of money and kept all of the rabbits, leased the rights at a low rental fee and split the profits made from the sale of the rabbits with the landowner, or was paid by the brace according to the number of rabbits killed after handing them over to the head gamekeeper or land agent. It goes without saying that a trapping contractor could make quite a lucrative income from the sale of rabbit meat to local people, butchers and game dealers and by selling the skins to furriers. However, he was not always a particularly popular man with tenant farmers or gamekeepers as he invariably left a residual stock of rabbits on the ground for breeding purposes in order to ensure that he had work available in the following season.

Contract trapping

George Leaning, a gamekeeper's son, left Normanby School in Lincolnshire in 1926. He secured temporary employment as a mole catcher with Mr Yuill, a trapping contractor who operated over a number of local estates. In his first three months, he caught a total of 1,059 moles. Thereafter he joined Mr Yuill on a permanent basis as a rabbit and mole trapper, remaining with him until the outbreak of the World War Two. He recalls that each trapper (three were employed) was responsible for working eighty mole traps, ninety-six rabbit traps and 200 snares. His employer charged customers 3d (1¼p) per acre for mole catching, but could sell moleskins to fur dealers for between 1d (½p) to 1/- (5p), according to the quality. Rabbits were taken in part payment for trapping services and were sold to local butchers and game dealers.

The truffle hunter

The truffle, a small edible fungi about the size of a golf ball, which grows underground in beechwood plantations on chalky downlands was a much sought after delicacy in parts of southern England until the early years of the twentieth century. Traditionally collected by itinerant woodmen, with the aid of a specially trained 'truffle hunting dog', truffles were harvested between the months of November and March, then either sold to private customers or sent up to the local country house for consumption by the landowner and his sporting guests.

In the Wiltshire village of Winterslow, several miles distant from Salisbury, truffle hunting was carried out on a semi-professional basis during the winter months by male members of the Bray, Collins and Yeats families from the eighteenth century until about 1930. These men, usually coppice workers or hurdle makers, went out on an almost daily basis in pursuit of the fungi in the extensive local woodlands, using a locally developed strain of long-haired Spanish poodle, known as a 'Winterslow truffle hunting dog', to sniff them out and to dig them up.

On a good day such a dog could detect and locate as many as 25lb of truffles. One of the largest truffles ever found by a dog, weighing more than 2lb, was sent by its owner, Eli Collins, to Queen Victoria, who rewarded him with a golden sovereign.

The Winterslow truffle hunting dogs eventually came to the attention of King Edward VII, who summoned Thomas Yeats, one of the leading hunters, to meet him at Highclere Castle in Hampshire while he was on a shooting visit to the Earl of Carnarvon. Yeats not only gave the King and his entourage a demonstration of truffle hunting in the Highclere woods but entertained them with an account of his truffle hunting experiences!

Yeats was one of only a handful of Winterslow men to continue hunting truffles with dogs into the twentieth century. Following his death in 1915, the sole surviving truffle hunter in the village was Alfred Newton Collins, who also worked as a woodman, firewood dealer and general labourer.

As well as hunting for truffles in and around Winterslow, Alfred Newton Collins travelled as far afield as Arundel in Sussex in pursuit of the fungi, often taking his hunting dogs by train to distant destinations. He either sold his truffles locally, or dispatched them by post in shoeboxes to clients in London and other towns and cities. In the early 1920s he was selling truffles at 2/6d (12½p) per lb.

Collins gave up truffle hunting about 1930 when he was in his late fifties. He was almost certainly the last man to breed and work Winterslow truffle hunting dogs. Sadly, as far as can be ascertained, these interesting and unusual dogs had become extinct by the 1940s.

The itinerant water supply craftsman

In the days before mains water was readily available, landowners employed a variety of itinerant craftsmen to locate and harness water sources for household and agricultural purposes on a country estate. The water diviner or 'dowser' would be called in to find the nearest underground spring or stream, using his divining rod, if a new cottage or farm building was being constructed in order that a well could be dug to provide a water supply. If water was required for sheep or cattle in the downland areas of Sussex, Hampshire, Wiltshire and a number of other counties, the dew pond maker would be contracted to dig a shallow, saucer-shaped dew pond, lined with puddled clay, straw and chalk rubble, to collect rainwater and dew. In areas where working water meadow systems were operated to increase agricultural productivity, the drowner would be hired in early spring to carry out controlled irrigation from a nearby river, not only to enable the river water to keep frosts off the grass but also to allow the ground to absorb plant nutrients and fertile silt carried by the water. He might also be taken on in a dry summer to irrigate the meadows to keep the grass growing.

Cattle refreshing themselves at the dew pond near Chanctonbury Ring, West Sussex, c1910. Dew pond making was a skilled craft, often passed down from father to son

Thomas Boughton – travelling artist

Thomas Boughton c1880.

Throughout the Victorian period the travelling artist was a familiar figure in the rural community visiting each village, country estate or large farmhouse on his patch once or twice a year in order to paint portraits of people, animals or landscapes. These men, many of whom were self-taught, performed a valuable function at a time when photography was still in its infancy and a visit to a photographer usually meant a time-consuming journey to a studio in the nearest town. Many examples of the work of these little-known artists survive today in local museums or art galleries or in private hands, providing a unique record in colour of social life in the countryside in days gone by.

Thomas Boughton was a well-known travelling artist in the Guildford district of Surrey from the late 1830s until the early 1890s. The son of a brewer, he was born at Woolwich in Kent in 1812 and spent much of his childhood and early teenage years at Thames Ditton on the edge of London, then a quiet Surrey village. From an early age he showed artistic talent and knew that he wanted to be a painter. However, his father insisted that he served a seven-year apprenticeship as a house painter, gilder, carver and decorator so that he would have a trade to fall back upon whenever his earnings as an artist were not enough to sustain him.

Upon completion of his apprenticeship in the early 1830s, Thomas set up in business as a self-employed house decorator in Guildford, painting in his spare time, particularly animals. His talents were soon recognised by various members of the local gentry, who commissioned him to paint dogs, horses or prize farm animals. Word of his ability to paint horses reached the ears of Lord Petre, who invited him to spend a few weeks at his Essex home, Thorndon Hall, to produce a set of paintings of his hunters and foxhounds. This resulted in a number of commissions for other equestrian-based portraits from friends of Lord Petre.

In the early 1840s, now working full-time as an artist, Thomas turned his attentions to painting birds both wild and game, using dead specimens as models. He proved to be very successful at this line in art, exhibiting four beautifully detailed paintings of dead game birds at the Royal Society of British Artists in London between 1845 and 1847. He had probably reached the peak of his career as a painter at this point.

By 1851, with a young family to support, Thomas had reverted to life as a painter and decorator, employing one man and an apprentice in order to allow him enough time to carry out art commissions on a limited basis. He was concentrating mainly on landscape painting at this period in his life. He painted a number of scenes in the vicinity of the Basingstoke canal, a series of pictures of sailing ships at sea, as well as portraits of various Guildford buildings, one of which depicting a view of the High Street now hangs in the town's art gallery.

Thomas frequently travelled by foot, on horseback or in the Carriers wagon (horse-drawn bus) to country estates or outlying villages within a 10-mile radius of Guildford in order to paint minor squires, farmers, senior country house servants such as butlers or head gamekeepers, or birds and animals. He was usually away from home for several days at a time, staying overnight in village inns, farmhouses, or in the servants' quarters at 'the big house'. In some instances he made sketches of his subject that he took back to his studio, where they were used as the basis for a painting. More often than not, though, he produced his portraits on the spot. Towards the end of his life he used photographs as well as sketches in preparation for a good quality painting, taking a professional photographer along with him to capture the scene or subject on a series of small *cartes de visit*.

Many of Thomas's paintings were done on old sail canvases or on ancient oak panels, which were then being ripped out of local country houses. He only purchased new canvas for expensive paintings. In addition to mixing his own oil paints from a selection of raw materials, he often gilded the frames in which his paintings were mounted. Rarely did he charge more than a few pounds for any picture. When he was short of work he painted signs featuring popular names of pubs, such as the 'George and the Dragon' or 'The Queens Head', which were easily saleable to village publicans.

In a self-portrait, believed to have been painted in the 1870s or '80s, Thomas depicts himself as a dignified man with a cut away beard, wearing a wide-brimmed black hat complemented by a black artist's smock. He is standing in a relaxed manner, paintbrush in hand, with a palette and easel to his left. Thomas Boughton continued to paint until shortly before his death in 1893. Many of his paintings survive today in private collections. Indeed, a bird picture fetched more than £1,000 when it was recently sold at a Surrey auction.

Oil painting of a curly coated retriever carrying a dead pheasant by Thomas Boughton c1840s.

14

THE RARE AND UNUSUAL

SOME WEALTHY LANDOWNERS employed an eclectic range of 'curiosities' among their outdoor service staff in times past, particularly if they had a special interest or hobby, ran a small estate business, or were of a somewhat eccentric disposition. In addition to hermits, agisters, menagerie keepers and decoy men, which were all generally fairly thin on the ground or found only in certain parts of the country, there were a number of one-offs such as the aviary keeper appointed by the 2nd Earl of Iveagh at Elveden in Suffolk, the master cheese maker from Somerset who was recruited by the 2nd Duke of Westminster to manage a dedicated cheese dairy at Eaton Hall in Cheshire and the golf professional and team of greenkeepers engaged by the 6th Duke of Portland to run the eighteen-hole private golf course at Nottinghamshire. Perhaps the most unusual post of all, however, that of the swannery keeper employed by the Earls of Ilchester and their successors to look after the colony of mute swans at Abbotsbury in Dorset, continues to be occupied today.

George Moss – custodian of Old Basing House

George Moss performed the somewhat unusual role of acting as the custodian of the ruins of Old Basing House on the Hackwood Park estate in Hampshire. Engaged by the 3rd Lord Bolton in 1872, he had previously worked as a sieve maker and as a carpenter, had spent a year in Canada and had served as a soldier in the Royal Horse Artillery during the Crimean War. Educated at a dame school and, later, at a night school organised by the local vicar, he not only gave guided walks and talks to members of the public visiting the ruins, but also superintended the extensive excavations that were carried out on the site by Lord Bolton over a period of several decades. He was held in such high esteem by the Bolton family that when he died in 1912 the 4th Lord Bolton paid for a headstone for his grave, which bears the inscription: 'In memory of George Moss, for many years custodian of Old Basing House, a faithful and trustworthy servant who died June 11th 1912 aged 79 years. This stone was erected by Lord Bolton.'

Opposite: Swannery keeper on the Abbotsbury estate, Dorset, c1910.

The menagerie keeper

The man in charge of the collection of exotic birds and animals that many eighteenth and nineteenth century landed proprietors kept to entertain their guests, the menagerie keeper might be expected to look after anything from an aviary of parrots to a herd of buffalo in a landscaped park. More often than not, he came under the control of the head gamekeeper and doubled either as an under-keeper or as a part-time park keeper as and when required.

Estate menageries varied tremendously in size and content depending upon the whims of the owner. For example, on the Rushmore estate in Wiltshire in the late Victorian period, the menagerie belonging to the well-known archaeologist General Augustus Pitt-Rivers included llamas, yaks, prairie dogs and reindeer as well as emus, Australian bower birds and South American parrots. This was in addition to various species of British cattle and foreign deer that he tried to hybridise. At Vaynol Park in Carnarvonshire, George Asheton Smith, who owned the property from 1869 until 1904, not only had herds of American bison and semi-wild British white cattle, but also boasted monkeys, lions bears and seals (which lived in a specially constructed 'seal pond') in his menagerie. On the Eaton estate in Cheshire during the 1930s, the 2nd Duke of Westminster, one of the last landowners to have a menagerie, kept Himalayan monkeys on an island in the fishpond in the Eaton Hall gardens along with a pair of pelicans and a small collection of ornamental wildfowl to add a dash of colour to things.

Male peacock in all his finery in the walled garden of a country house. Peacocks were a popular menagerie bird.

The 'hermit's cell' or hermitage at Badminton, Gloucestershire, c1910.

The hermit

Fashionable during the eighteenth and the early nineteenth centuries, the hermit, otherwise known as an 'ornamental hermit' or a 'garden hermit', was employed to amuse guests on estates belonging to wealthy members of the aristocracy and the landed gentry. Expected to dress like a druid, with long flowing hair and beard, and unkempt fingernails, he was provided with a purpose-built 'hermit's cell' in the form of a hermitage, a folly or a grotto, which was usually situated in a landscaped park or on a hilltop, and had to remain permanently on site in order that he could be viewed for entertainment or consulted for some sage advice. In return for living such a Spartan lifestyle, he was paid a small annual salary and, according to some contemporary accounts, had his meals sent out to him from the mansion by a manservant.

Seen as something of an extravagance by the Victorians, the practice of retaining a hermit had by and large ceased by the mid-nineteenth century. That said, during the Edwardian era the 9th Duke of Beaufort occasionally instructed his second footman to put on a false beard, pretend to be a hermit and to sit in the hermit's cell on the Badminton estate in Gloucestershire in order that guests could go and peer at him!

Arthur Moody, falconer and head bird keeper to the 5th Lord Lilford at Lilford Hall, Oundle, Northamptonshire, 1905.

The falconer

Professional falconers were employed on a handful of country estates from the mid-Victorian period until the outbreak of World War Two by landowners who were hawking enthusiasts – many of whom belonged to the Old Hawking Club founded in the early 1860s. Highly specialised men, they managed the Mews (hawk house) where the falcons were kept, trained and worked the birds, and would accompany their master to hawking meetings in various parts of Great Britain to hawk partridges, red grouse, rooks, crows, magpies, rabbits and other species of game and vermin.

The agister

Originally an official appointed by the monarch to manage the cattle kept by commoners and others in the royal forests of England, the agister could also be found on a number of large country estates until the late Victorian period. His principal duties involved looking after cattle, horses and other livestock belonging to employees, tenants and others kept in the park – where they often roamed alongside the deer, collecting the agistment fees paid for the use of the pasturage and keeping an eye on the owners when they visited their stock to ensure they did not undertake unauthorised activities such as poaching or gathering nuts, berries and firewood. In some instances, the head gamekeeper or the park keeper acted as agister, thereby preventing a conflict of interests between game preservation and agistment, delegating the day-to-day work to an under-keeper, a stockman or a farm labourer.

Agistment, or 'joisting' as the practice was often known, was traditionally carried out between May and October in order that tenant farmers could graze their cattle in an estate park, thus freeing their own fields for hay production. It was usual, however, for a specific area of a park to be set aside throughout the year for the use of estate employees who did not have any land other than a garden.

Bullock in a parkland setting c1910.

The 6th Duke of Devonshire, for example, provided agistment facilities for both employees and tenants in his 1,100 acre park at Chatsworth in Derbyshire, as James Caird notes in *English Agriculture In 1850–51*:

> The park itself is partly devoted to the villagers' comfort, the best of it being reserved for the cows of the cottagers and labourers on the estate. The rates

paid by the labourers for joisting a cow are from 50/- (£2.50) to 55/- (£2.55), which are very moderate, and must add much to the comfort of a labourer's fireside.

Another part of the park, about 300 acres in extent, is joisted to the tenants, who are thereby enabled to ease their farms of young stock in summer, and to reserve part of their grass for hay. The rate charged to the farmers for year-olds is 25/- (£1.05); for two year olds, 35/- (£1.55); for young horses, 50/- (£2.50) each; and for a mare and a foal, £5. We are persuaded that this is a plan which might be advantageously adopted on many large estates, and which would afford, on moderate terms, very useful keep for the neighbouring tenantry, and possibly with more direct advantage to the proprietor than he, on average, secures from speculating in the grazing of cattle on his own account.

Estate accounts for Hackwood Park in Hampshire dating back to the same period record that in April 1854, John Bond, the head gamekeeper, park keeper, bailiff of the in-hand land and agister, collected the sum of £22-9/-3d (£22.46½) for cattle taken into the park. Cows were charged at 2/- (10p) per week, but fees for horses varied. Pigs belonging to estate employees could be kept in the park free of charge during the pannage season from September to December and were looked after collectively by boys, who were paid 1/- (5p) a week.

Although no longer found on large country estates with extensive areas of parkland, agisters continue to be employed today in the New Forest in Hampshire, where they carry out the day-to-day duties of administering the forest and assist in the management of livestock belonging to commoners.

Fritton decoy, Norfolk, c1920.

The decoy man

Found on estates in eastern England and elsewhere from the late seventeenth century until the outbreak of World War One, the decoy man operated the decoy, which was used to catch ducks and other wildfowl for the table and for sale on the open market. His principal task involved enticing or decoying ducks into decoy pipes, structures covered with netting situated over ditches running off the edge of a lake, using a specially trained 'decoy dog' and killing the ducks thereafter. He either worked directly for the landowner and was usually accountable to the head gamekeeper or rented the decoy rights and built and ran his own decoy. Today, the handful of working decoys that remain are used for duck ringing rather than for food procurement purposes.

Wretham decoy

Situated on the Wretham estate in Norfolk, the Wretham decoy continued to be operated by the head gamekeeper, Mr Brown, during and after World War One. The naturalist, Joseph Rainer, who visited Wretham in July 1918, while making an authoritative survey of British duck decoys, provides this description of the decoy:

> Common wild ducks are principally the ducks taken, but teal, widgeon, shovellers and gadwall are caught now and again. The piece of water is known as the Mickle Mere and is situated in Wretham Park, midway between Thetford and Watton. It is now about eighty years since the decoy was made. One of the good seasons was 1883–84, when 1,640 ducks was taken. A decoy book was started in 1868. It is found here that a good year for acorns is a poor year for taking ducks, for the ducks then leave the water continually to go into the plantations to feed on them. Teal and widgeon are not often taken, though there are frequently many hundreds on the water. This is now the only decoy worked in Norfolk; formerly there were twenty one and in 1886 there were five. The following are some of the best years lately:
> 1896–97, 1,807; 1897–98, 935; 1900–01, 1,354; 1903–04, 881; 1906–07, 1,259; 1907–08, 806; 1908–09, 950; 1910–11, 711; 1913–14, 1,283; 1915–16, 992.

The railwayman

Employed to operate and maintain the private narrow gauge railway system found on a handful of country estates during the late nineteenth and the early twentieth centuries, the railwayman was a multi-skilled individual who was capable of driving and maintaining the locomotives, acting as guard and goods porter or carrying out track maintenance duties. For instance, the driver–engineer on the Eaton estate railway in Cheshire was responsible for looking after two steam locomotives and a petrol engine along with a fleet of trucks and carriages that were used to transport goods and passengers between the Great Western Railway station at Balderton and Eaton Hall, a distance of around 3 miles. His colleague, the guard, undertook the various other tasks involved in running a train safely and manned the ungated level crossings on the line as and when necessary. The network came under the control of the head forester, who doubled as superintendent of the line, ensuring that the track was maintained on a regular basis by the forestry department staff, that the associated fences and hedges were kept in good order and that the necessary train movement records were kept.

The Sand Hutton Light Railway

Constructed by Sir Robert Walker, Bt., in the early 1920s to serve the 10,000 acre Sand Hutton estate in North Yorkshire, the 18in gauge Sand Hutton Light Railway connected Sand Hutton Hall to Warthill Station on the York–Beverley–Hull line of the North Eastern Railway. The railway ran for just over 5 miles, including a branch line to Claxton brickworks, and not only conveyed goods and supplies for the estate but also transported bricks from the brickworks and potatoes, sugar beet, hay and other outgoing produce from the tenant farms. It also carried fare-paying passengers on Wednesdays and Saturdays in two specially built carriages. In addition to five stations, four halts and transhipment sidings at Warthill, where incoming and outgoing freight was transferred from mainline wagons to Sand Hutton rolling stock, a locomotive depot and repair shop was provided at White Sike Junction to house and maintain the fleet of four steam engines used to haul the trains. Managed by Sir Robert's land agent at Sand Hutton, S.C. Foster, who acted as secretary and general manager, the railway was controlled on a day-to-day basis by the estate engineer, George Batty, also the senior driver, who was responsible for the operating staff consisting of a driver, a guard and three or four goods porters. The railway itself and the associated buildings were kept in tip-top condition by the estate yard building team.

Estate engineer, George Batty, driving locomotive No 12 on the Sand Hutton estate railway 1927.

Notwithstanding the large amount of freight carried on behalf of paying customers, the Sand Hutton Light Railway was extremely costly to operate and maintain throughout the period of its existence. Two years after Sir Robert Walker's death in 1930 his Trustees closed the railway as it had become a burden on estate finances and sold the track, locomotives and rolling stock to a firm of Sheffield scrap merchants.

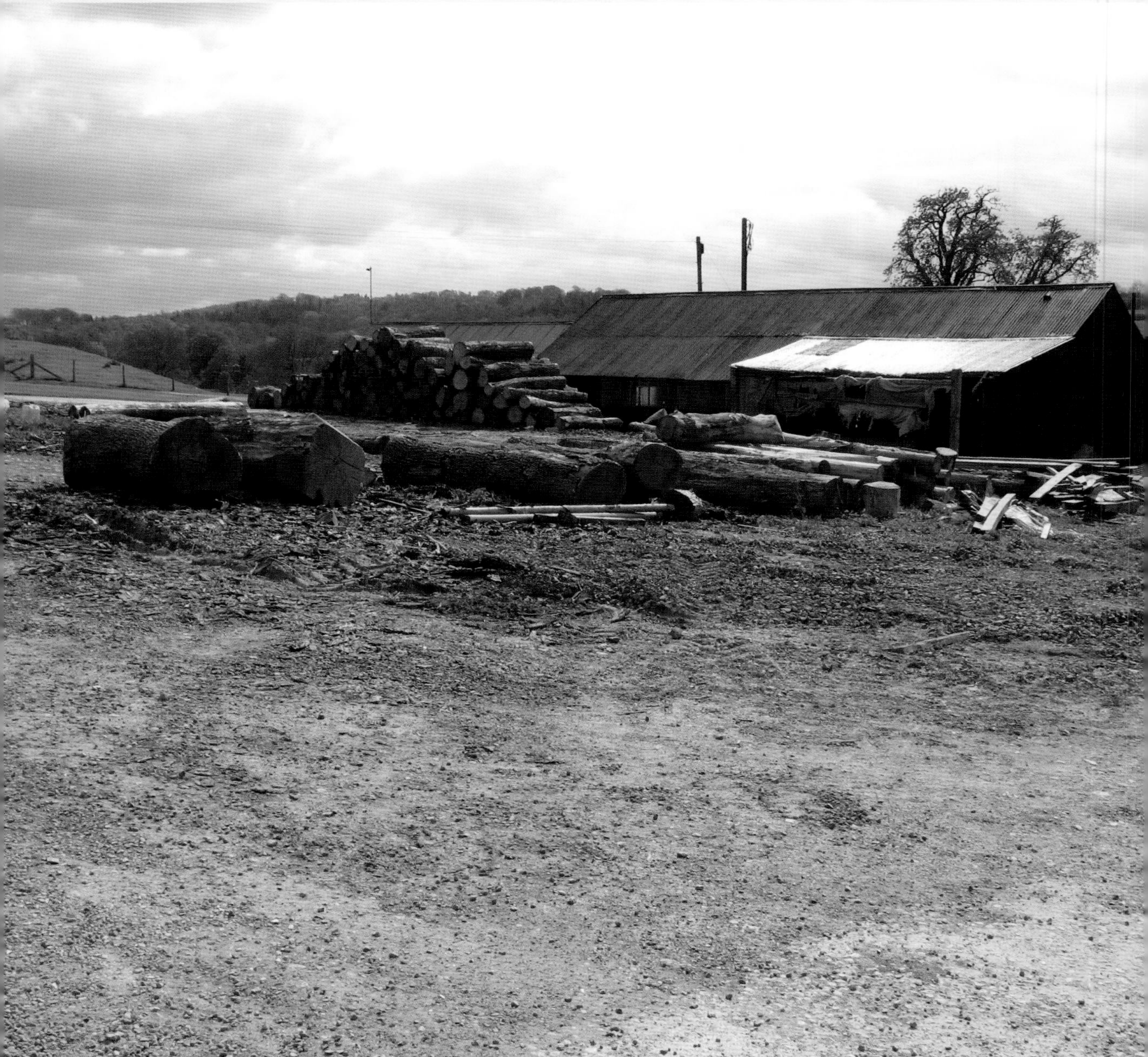

15

THE ESTATE YARD TEAM

THE ESTATE YARD team was responsible for carrying out new building work, property maintenance and general repairs on the country estate, both outdoors and indoors. Controlled by the clerk of works, who was directly accountable to the land agent, the team included a wide variety of tradesmen who could undertake virtually any task required from constructing a new farm building or extending part of the mansion to hanging a field gate or restoring a piece of antique furniture. Situated either adjacent to the service quarters of the mansion or a short distance away, the yard on a large estate would usually include a joinery workshop where doors, windows and other timber products were manufactured, a wood yard where home-grown timber was seasoned and processed, an engineering workshop and a blacksmiths' shop, a plumbers' workshop, staff mess rooms, storage facilities for carts, ladders and building materials and the clerk of works office. On some properties, the electric lighting plant and the electricians' workshop was also based in the estate yard, along with the private fire station.

It was not unusual for between fifty and 100 tradesmen and labourers to be employed in the estate yard on a country estate with a large stately home and a vast

Opposite: Home-grown timber stacked and awaiting processing in the wood yard section of the estate yard at Fonthill, Wiltshire, 2017.

Left: Tradesmen and labourers on a Surrey estate c1890. Men such as these were capable of undertaking a multitude of tasks ranging from hanging a field gate to restoring a church.

acreage of land during the Victorian and the Edwardian periods, all of whom carried out their work manually using hand tools. Some ducal establishments kept whole armies of men to improve and maintain their property. The 7th Duke of Bedford, for example, retained a staff of 300 craftsmen at Woburn Abbey in Bedfordshire in the 1840s, all of whom were paid on a weekly basis. Even as late as the 1920s when landowners throughout the country were scaling down estate operations due to high taxation and rising labour costs, Sir Berkeley Sheffield, Bt., continued to employ around fifty-two men in the estate yard at Normanby Park in Lincolnshire!

Members of the estate yard team were invariably provided with a tied cottage on the estate, free fuel and perquisites of one kind or another. The men were generally paid less than self-employed tradesmen, but had job security for life. Indeed, many followed the same occupation on the same property on a father-to-son basis for several generations.

The clerk of works

Estate carpenter on his way to carry out outdoor repair work c1910. In addition to building maintenance, these men regularly undertook hedge carpentry duties, which involved installing or repairing gates, fences, footbridges over rivers or streams and similar tasks.

The manager of the estate yard team, the clerk of works was responsible for keeping the mansion, the farms, cottages and all other buildings on the country estate in good order, as well as for maintaining the boundary walls, the gates, the fences and the driveways. He and his staff undertook new building work as and when necessary, working under the supervision of a hired architect on all major projects. Together with the land agent, he inspected all of the principal estate buildings, the workers' houses and the rented properties on a routine basis, usually every four to seven years depending on the whims of the landowner, and arranged for repainting to be carried out and for any worn-out doors, windows or other fixtures to be replaced. In addition to the usual building tradesman, the clerk of works on a large estate might have a plasterer, a glazier, a cabinetmaker, an upholsterer and a gang of roadmen on his team, as well as a secretary and a bookkeeper to assist him with administration duties.

The carpenter

A multi-talented individual who could turn his hand to virtually any woodworking task, the carpenter either worked permanently in the joinery workshop at the estate yard where he made doors, windows and other items, or travelled around the estate undertaking repairs or installing new fixtures in buildings under construction. He was expected to be able produce any timber product required on a country property, ranging from field gates and cow stalls to elm water pipes and coffins manufactured from home-grow oak. He sometimes glazed windows and did small painting jobs, too.

The house carpenter

The house carpenter worked within the mansion carrying out any repairs that were required to the internal fixtures made out of wood or to the furnishings. More skilled than the ordinary estate carpenter, he was not only expected to produce high-quality replacement items as and when needed, but also to be able to make simple furniture, picture frames and wooden toys for his employer's children at Christmas and other times. On some properties the house carpenter was a fully qualified cabinetmaker, capable of undertaking extremely intricate tasks that normally warranted specialist attention.

The sawyer

Based in the wood yard, the sawyer converted trees felled on a country estate into lengths of timber suitable for construction purposes. Standing on top of a tree trunk laid across a sawpit, a kind of small open cellar dug out of the ground, he and his mate, known as the 'bottom sawyer', cut up the trunk into a plank or a beam by hand with a double-handled pit saw. The plank or beam would then be seasoned in an open shed for several years until deemed fit for carpentry use. Pit sawing was gradually superseded by steam- or water-powered mechanical sawing machinery during the late nineteenth century, with the result that the sawyer became a machine operator.

Above: Upholsterer repairing a chair in a country house c1905. In times past, a number of large estates, including Belvoir in Leicestershire and Chatsworth in Derbyshire, employed a full-time upholsterer in the carpentry department.

Left: Sawyers converting a newly felled tree into 'green' building timber ready for seasoning using mobile mechanical sawing machinery powered by a steam traction engine c1910.

The stone mason

One of the key members of the estate yard team, the stonemason was responsible for maintaining the exterior stone work of the mansion, for restoring or making replacement cornices, carvings and other facing features that adorned the outside of the mansion, the gate lodges and the follies, and for keeping the terraces, pavements and statuary in the gardens and parkland in good order. He also repaired any wet stone boundary walls on an estate.

The drystone walling gang

Found on country estates in the north of England, the Peak District, the Cotswolds, Wales and other regions where stone rather than brick was used for general construction purposes, the drystone walling gang built and maintained the stone walls that surrounded the fields and the woods and sometimes carried out repairs to barns and to shooting boxes, stone tracks and stone-lined drains on grouse moors. On a large property with miles of walls, it was usual for several walling gangs to be employed on a full-time basis, although some cost-conscious landowners engaged itinerant contractors to carry out their walling work.

Dry stone wallers at work on an estate in the north of England, 1932.

The bricklayer

Generally less skilled than the stone mason, the bricklayer undertook building work within the mansion, constructed, extended and repaired farms and cottages on an estate and maintained any brick garden or boundary walls. Some bricklayers also carried out basic plastering work and external rendering of buildings as well as retiling roofs.

Plumber's workshop in the Lockinge estate yard, Oxfordshire' c1950. *Courtesy of the Lockinge Trust Estate*

The plumber

Not only responsible for looking after the pipe work that conveyed the water supply around the mansion and for the central heating system, if any, the plumber also carried out lead roofing work as and when necessary. Based in his own workshop in the estate yard, he made pipe fittings, roof furniture, chimney flashings and any other lead products required for building or estate purposes.

The electrician

Something of a newcomer to the estate yard team, the electrician maintained the electric lighting plant, which many progressive landowners began to install at mansions from the late Victorian period onwards. In addition to operating the plant, he carried out wiring repairs and minor alterations to the supply system and changed light bulbs when required. Sometimes also known as the 'engineer', the electrician at a minor country house frequently doubled as the chauffeur!

Estate painters posing for the camera with a maid in a painting cage outside a country mansion c1905. The cage was lowered down the side of the building by ropes secured to the roof to enable men to paint the upper windows.

The painter and decorator

The painter and decorator carried out all of the interior and exterior decorating work required both for the mansion and for the numerous buildings on a country estate. He made his own paints from lead, chemicals and other raw materials, and manufactured the paste he used for hanging wallpaper. In addition to painting the outside of all the farms and cottages on the property in the 'estate colours' – often a dark brown, red, green or blue – every few years, he painted all the gates on the driveways white on a regular basis so they were visible to coachmen, chauffeurs and other travellers at night. He might also be sent to London out of season from time to time to decorate his employer's town house.

The general building labourer

Building labourers manually dredging a pond in a deer park c1910. After being dug out by shovel, the silt is transferred by wheelbarrow to a spoil heap prior to removal from the site by horse-drawn cart.

Employed by the estate yard department to carry out heavy manual work on building and maintenance projects or to act as an assistant or 'mate' to a particular tradesman, the general building labourer sometimes also helped out in the gardens, on the home farm or with forestry operations at busy times. On more progressive estates, an intelligent labourer often had the opportunity to learn a trade after several years' service and was given appropriate on the job training.

The Lockinge Estate Yard Team

Established in the mid-Victorian period when the 1st Lord and Lady Wantage acquired the manors and freehold land of Ardington, Lockinge and the surrounding area in order to form the 20,500 acre Lockinge estate in Oxfordshire, the Lockinge estate yard employed more than 100 craftsmen and labourers in its heyday during the early years of the twentieth century. The men were not only responsible for the maintenance of Lockinge House, numerous tenant farms and a dozen or so villages, but also restored churches and rectories on the estate, built new village schools, constructed new farm buildings as and when required and totally rebuilt several villages in the distinctive 'Lockinge style' of estate architecture. Estate yard facilities included a timber yard, carpenters, blacksmiths, plumbers and other workshops, along with a clerk of works office.

Notwithstanding the high taxation imposed upon landowners during the post-World War One era, together with the changing land management practices and staff reductions that were implemented on country estates between the 1920s and the 1950s the Lockinge estate yard continued to employ twenty-eight men in 1961, including nine carpenters (some of whom were formerly wheelwrights) three bricklayers, five painters and decorators, two plumbers, a blacksmith, a lorry driver, storekeeper, four general labourers and two part-time old age pensioners. Remarkably, the estate yard still operates today, a rare survivor from a bygone era, but now the team of craftsmen undertake private building commissions from members of the public in addition to carrying out all the maintenance and building work throughout the estate and providing commercial facilities for servicing and repairing agricultural machinery in the engineering workshops.

Blacksmith at work in the Lockinge estate yard blacksmith's shop c1950.
Courtesy of the Lockinge Trust Estate

The riding school at Welbeck Abbey, Nottinghamshire, c1905. Some of the more prestigious estates had a riding school, which was not only used for tuition purposes but also for riding and exercising horses in adverse weather conditions.

$$\text{16}$$

COUNTRY HOUSE SERVICES

PRIOR TO THE outbreak of World War One, few large country estates depended upon public utilities of any kind, even if available in the area. Many operated as a self-contained unit with their own private water and sewage works, waste disposal facilities, electric lighting plant or gas works, post room and telegraph office (in effect a private sub-post office) and a fire brigade staffed by trained volunteers from various departments. The great majority of establishments also had a private church or chapel with a resident priest and some maintained an estate school for the children of staff members, originally provided in pre-state education days.

Specialist staff were employed to maintain these services, although a chauffeur or a member of the estate yard team often doubled as the lighting plant engineer and an odd job man or labourer usually acted as the refuse collector. Skilled men were also kept to maintain the state of the art leisure facilities such as polo grounds, swimming pools, tennis courts and riding schools that were added at Welbeck Abbey, Lilleshall Hall and other grand country houses during the late Victorian and the Edwardian periods. In addition, large properties invariably retained one or two full-time window cleaners and a night watchman who was responsible for security at night-time and for keeping a look out for fire.

Holy Trinity Church, Alltyferin, Carmarthenshire, 1939. Built in 1865 as a private church for the owner of the Alltyferin estate, Henry Bath, to serve as a place of worship for his family and servants, it is now used by the local community.

The fire brigade

Many of the wealthier landowners with prestigious country houses filled with valuable works of art and other treasures started to become 'fire conscious' in the second half of the nineteenth century. They not only installed primitive extinguishing appliances and fitted outside fire escapes in discreet locations, but also formed private estate fire brigades to counteract the risk of a blaze in buildings heated with coal and lit by candles, oil lamps or gas. In addition, indoor and

151

The estate fire brigade at Elveden, Suffolk, with their steam-powered fire engine and wheeled fire escape, 1914.

outdoor servants were trained to be on the lookout for the first signs of a potential conflagration either in the house itself or the adjoining outbuildings, to raise the alarm and to seek help to tackle the root of the fire wherever possible.

Estate fire brigades generally consisted of volunteers drawn from various outdoor departments, although at Dupplin Castle in Perthshire the Earl of Kinnoull formed a brigade made up entirely of gamekeepers. The firemen came under the command of a captain or chief, usually a senior member of staff (at Badminton in Gloucestershire the 'chief fire officer' was the land agent), and a held a fire practice once a week for which they were often paid a small monthly bonus in addition to their wages. On some estates, a representative from Merryweathers, the fire protection engineers, visited once a year to drill the brigade and to check its equipment.

The firemen were issued with uniforms and brass helmets, which were kept in a dressing room or 'station', where hoses, ladders and other fire-fighting equipment would be stored. The dressing room would be situated in the stable yard or other outbuildings near to a country house and acted as an assembly point if a fire alarm was raised.

Fire brigades were invariably equipped with a hand-pulled or a horse-drawn fire engine manufactured by Merryweather or Shand Mason that was capable of pumping

water by hand or steam from a nearby lake or river to control and put out a fire. The engine was usually kept in a specially constructed 'fire engine house' in the stable yard, or occasionally beneath a large water tower.

In some instances, hydrant systems were installed in the grounds of a country house, either to provide a ready supply of water for the fire engine or for direct connection to fire hoses. These were often maintained and tested on a fortnightly basis by the gardeners. For example, the ultra-rich 4th Duke of Sutherland surrounded Lilleshall Hall, his Shropshire seat, with fire hydrants connected to a 6in main from his private water supply that ensured 'sufficient pressure to enable the throwing of a jet of water to the roof of the house'.

Landowners with large agricultural estates often owned two engines, one for their country house, the other for use on the farms, and sometimes donated an engine to the nearest village, which was crewed by local volunteers. The Earl of Scarborough, for example, maintained a steam-powered fire engine for use at Sandbeck Park, his Yorkshire seat, and a manual engine for the farms, which apparently consisted of a long box-like affair on four wheels and took eight men to operate, who pumped for all they were worth on long handles to put out a haystack fire.

The great majority of estate fire brigades were disbanded after the outbreak of

Manually operated fire engine similar to that in use at Sandbeck Park in Yorkshire. Engines of this kind were used to extinguish or contain farm fires …

Stack Fire at Catfield 4/11/11

... such as the haystack fire pictured here at Catfield in Norfolk in 1911.

World War One due to staff shortages and were not re-formed following the cessation of hostilities in 1918 owing to financial constraints and the increasing availability of local authority fire services in all rural areas. That said, engines often remained in situ in outbuildings for many years before being scrapped or refurbished as a 'curiosity' for modern day stately home visitors!

First aid training

The 4th Countess Manvers broke new ground in country house circles in 1912 by organising a series of lectures on 'how to render first aid to the injured' in order to train the servants and tenants on the Thoresby estate in Nottinghamshire in such procedures. She subsequently formed the Thoresby Branch of the St John Ambulance Association and issued a 'Notice in Case of Accidents', which was given to members and others and placed in strategic locations around the estate:

A stretcher and stores will be found in the Thoresby wood yard in a room labelled 'Ambulance', and also stores at Thoresby House in the Fire Appliance Room; a stretcher and stores will also be kept in the Budby Reading Room, and any member – or other person, if a member is not available – is at liberty to take the key from the glass box near the door in case of emergency, but must report to Mr Spink (secretary) any instance of first aid rendered and stores used. In the case of an accident happening requiring the use of a conveyance, application for such conveyance must be made to the person in charge at Thoresby stables.

Opposite (top): Advertisement for Hancock & Rixon electric lighting plant for country house use, 1911.

Opposite (bottom): Interior of a country house power station showing the water-powered dynamo equipment and the control panels, 1911.

The electric lighting plant

In 1878 the eminent Victorian industrialist, engineer and scientist, Lord Armstrong, pioneered the use of electric lighting in a country house, installing a hydro-electrically powered arc lamp in the gallery at Cragside, his state of the art mansion in Northumberland. Two years later in 1880 he installed an electric lighting system throughout the house, using incandescent lamps invented by Joseph Swan. He subsequently fitted an electrically powered lift, a primitive electric dishwasher, an electrically driven roasting spit and electric dinner gongs in order to make life easier for his household staff.

Landowners were initially slow to install electric lighting due to the costs involved but by the early 1900s many country houses both large and small had an electric plant of one kind or another. Lighting plants at this time were generally powered by a water-driven dynamo, a gas engine or an oil engine, all of which charged accumulator batteries that fed electricity into the lighting circuits. The plant at The Grange at Alresford in Hampshire, for instance, typical of that used to supply a grand house during the Edwardian era, was housed in a purpose-built power station and consisted of two 25hp Hornsby engines and two 110 volt dynamos with a switchboard and storage batteries.

The electric lighting plant on a large estate would be maintained by a full-time chief engineer or chief electrician, assisted by a small team of engineers or electricians who also changed light bulbs and carried out wiring repairs or alterations as and when necessary. On a smaller property, the plant was often the responsibility of a chauffeur as Delmé Jones, whose father, Tom, was chauffeur to Captain T.P. Lewes at Llanayron in Cardiganshire during the early 1930s, recounts:

My father had to maintain the private electric light system, a dynamo which was set in a shed by the water wheel which drove it and charged a number of accumulators which were housed in a room in the stable yard. The current was carried by overhead wires from the dynamo to the battery shed. In case for some reason the water wheel was unable to work, a small Petter oil engine had been installed in the dynamo shed as an alternative source of power. The water wheel was also used to provide power for sawing timber and operating the hay grabs for lifting the hay out of the carts at hay harvest time. Only the mansion and stable yard were lit by electric. Charging during the winter months went on daily from about 9 am to 1 pm. If for some reason father had to go out, another member of staff was requisitioned to keep an eye on things.

Some country estates continued to generate their own electricity for lighting and power purposes until the 1950s, when ease of access to the National Grid in the more remote rural areas made it economically unviable to operate a private power plant.

Estate telephone systems

Private telephone systems powered by the electric lighting plant were installed on a number of prestigious country estates during the Edwardian era in order to provide communication facilities around the mansion and the outbuildings. Lord Iveagh, owner of the celebrated Elveden sporting estate in Suffolk, even laid on an external system along one of the principal private roads with post-mounted sockets located at every mile to enable his gamekeeping staff to send regular progress reports back to the hall on a shoot day via a portable telephone instrument, which was carried in a car or a game cart. Impressed by such an innovative facility, a Canadian journalist visiting the property shortly before the outbreak of World War One told his readers:

Telephones and pheasants
Telephones connect all of the shooting butts at Elveden Hall, near Bury
St Edmunds, Norfolk, England, where King George went recently for
his customary shooting visit to the Earl of Iveagh. This 20,000 acre
preserve, where the King has gone shooting every fall for thirty years,

abounds in woodcock, partridge and pheasant, and the shoots are conducted in a most scientific manner. Every covert is connected up by a system of telephones to aid the bird-seekers. When game is flushed and missed by one Gun, it is possible immediately to telephone a nearby-shooter to be on his guard. Automobiles are used to convey the Guns from drive to drive for the different beats, and at noon motor-cars haul hot luncheons to that part of the wood where the sportsmen are assembled.

The clergyman

In times past, a resident Church of England clergyman was employed on most estates to act as vicar or chaplain of the private chapel in a great country house or the estate church in the grounds. His principal role was to hold a morning service each weekday for the benefit of the landowner, members of his family and many of his indoor and outdoor servants, to hold services on a Sunday and other religious occasions and to officiate at baptisms, weddings, funerals and other events. He might also combine his duties with those of tutor to his employer's children or as in-house librarian.

The clergyman was usually fairly closely related to his employer, often a younger brother, an uncle or an impecunious cousin and, more often than not, was chosen as much for his hunting, shooting and fishing skills as for his ability to preach. In many instances, he appointed senior outdoor servants on the estate as his churchwardens and invariably encouraged workers' wives to help out at church events.

If a landowner was a Roman Catholic rather than a member of the Church of England he would generally retain a resident priest to officiate in his private chapel or church and, wherever possible, recruit Catholics rather than Protestants as servants. Non-Conformist landowners, although few and far between, did not employ a resident minister but regularly held morning prayer meetings themselves for the benefit of their family and staff.

The estate school

Some of the more enlightened landowners established an estate school on their property during the first half of the nineteenth century to provide the children of their servants and tenants with a basic education. The Duke of Wellington started a school at Stratfield Saye in Hampshire, where the children of staff and tenants were educated free of charge, but which charged a fee of 8d (3p) per week to teach children without estate connections. Sir Harry Featherstonhaugh built a school at Harting in Sussex for the estate children at Uppark and the local villagers. Lady Crewe, the chatelaine of Calke Abbey in Derbyshire, opened Lady Crewe's Free School in 1822 specifically for the daughters of estate employees and not only offered a curriculum suitable for girls destined for domestic service, but found all her pupils a situation before they left and gave them an outfit of new clothes.

Landowners either employed a male school master to run an estate school if the roll was large, along with one or two local girls who acted as assistants or pupil–teachers, or an articulate local woman if numbers were small. The school master and his staff came under the management of the land agent, who was also responsible for controlling the finances and keeping the school in good order. In addition to teaching children, some school masters were expected to run evening classes to teach adult estate employees in the rudiments of reading, writing and arithmetic.

Following the passage of the Education Act of 1870, which paved the way for free state education for all children, the great majority of estate schools were taken over by the nearest local school board and funded by the local council. Landowners, however, continued to exercise a considerable amount of control over rural schools by sitting on school boards or acting as governors. Indeed, until the 1930s schools were openly encouraged to release pupils for seasonal estate work such as harvesting, potato picking and beating on shoot days. Pupils at Sandbeck in Yorkshire and at Hodnet in Shropshire were also given a half-day off to attend foxhound meets at the local 'big house'!

Bentley School, Worcestershire. Founded by local squire, Richard Hemming in the 1850s, the school was closed in 1960 then extended and given to the people of Bentley in 1962 by his great grandson, Colonel Leslie Gray-Cheape, for use as a village hall. The original dame school can be seen in the background.

Bentley School

The estate school at Bentley in Worcestershire was founded by the local squire, Richard Hemming, in the 1850s and continued to be financially supported by his descendants until it closed in 1960. Maudie Ellis, his granddaughter, provides a brief history of the school in her book, *The Squire of Bentley*:

> Bentley School was started by my grandfather to save the children the long tramp to Tardebigge. It was a dame's school, and a little black-and-white half-timbered cottage on the estate was set aside for the old lady, who taught the few children round her in the parlour. But the number soon outgrew the parlour, so the old squire built a small school close by, the cottage becoming the schoolmaster's house, as it is today. In 1898 the squire again enlarged the school building. All the expenses are still borne by the estate, and an average of fifty children attend, for it has been much appreciated by parents for many years, and children from far and near go to it.

Advertisement depicting a variety of pumps suitable for supplying water to country houses, estates and farms from wells and other sources, 1916.

17

PAY AND PERKS

HISTORICALLY, OUTDOOR SERVANTS were never particularly well paid but were certainly better off than unskilled agricultural labourers, who were often laid off during the winter months and obliged to seek refuge in the local workhouse; itinerant rural craftsmen, who frequently lived a nomadic lifestyle and camped out in a rough shack on the worksite; or factory workers in towns and cities, who were responsible for finding their own living expenses out of their wages.

In addition to receiving a cash wage, those employed in private service benefited from free accommodation, clothing, generous meals and a daily beer or cider allowance if living in the servants' quarters in a mansion or an estate bothy. If they were married they were provided with a rent-free cottage on a country estate, and a range of perks that varied according to the whims of a landowner, but usually included an annual supply of firewood, any necessary clothing and a brace of rabbits, hares or game birds two or three times during the shooting season. Some estates also provided healthcare facilities, pensions or annuities and retirement housing for long-serving employees. They also looked after widows with young families, letting them keep their home and paying them a small wage in return for a few hours' housework in the mansion every day. Servants of all grades invariably received a Christmas box of some description, either in cash or in kind, and an invitation to the annual servants' ball held early in the New Year after the household festivities had finished.

Recruitment

Landowners recruited their outdoor servants in a variety of ways. Some were recommended by friends, relatives or neighbouring landed proprietors and duly appointed without any kind of correspondence or interview. Others were taken on as school leavers and trained in a particular trade. Hunt servants, stable staff, gardeners, foresters, chauffeurs and gamekeepers were usually sourced through advertisements placed in *The Field*, *The Gamekeeper*, *Horse & Hound*, various gardening periodicals and local newspapers, or through specialist servants' employment agencies, and were engaged after suitable references had been received. Gamekeepers, in particular, tended to be recruited from out of the area so they were not related to local labourers,

Opposite: The outdoor servants on an unknown country estate c1910. Happy and well-fed, if not highly paid, they undoubtedly enjoyed a range of perks in addition to their wages.

farmers or poachers, all of whom could put them in a compromising position. Land agents and estate clergymen, interestingly, were often impecunious relatives of a landowner, impoverished members of the aristocracy and the landed gentry, or retired military officers with little means of support other than their service pension. Estate maintenance staff, woodmen and specialist farm workers were often recruited from local families living in estate villages, many of whom worked on the same property carrying out the same trade on a father-to-son basis.

Letter sent by Miss Gwendoline Lloyd Price, MFH, master of the privately owned Penylan Foxhounds in Carmarthenshire, to an applicant for the post of kennel boy at the Talardd hunt kennels outlining the work involved and the terms of employment:

Talardd,
Maesycrugiau,
Carmarthenshire

11th October, 1938

Dear Sir,
I am much obliged for your letter received yesterday. I can hardly think that this situation would suit you. What I want is a boy to clean kennels, boil meat and pudding, ride exercise, clean tack; 3 horses and 20 couple of hounds. Of course the kennel huntsman straps and cleans tack too and feeds – he whips-in and the boy mostly brings a horse to the meet and goes home early. Rough hunting country, no one out but occasional farmers. Wages £1 a week with a bedroom in a local farmhouse, feeding in the main house. You would find the establishment very small after Allteryferin – you could come down by bus one day and interview me if you wish, but I think you probably would not care about the work, unless you wished to start to qualify for a hunt establishment later on.

Yours faithfully
Gwendoline M. Lloyd Price

Employment contracts

Senior outdoor servants such as the land agent and the various departmental heads on a country estate either entered into a legally binding contractual agreement with a landowner prior to taking up employment or were issued with an informal letter of engagement detailing wages and emoluments and the duties expected, along with any periods of notice applicable to both parties. Gamekeepers and hunt servants of all levels generally had some kind of contract of employment, too, to prevent them from leaving on the spot and disrupting their master's sporting programme. Farm staff were usually hired annually, although many remained on the same estate for years on end. Some other servants, particularly those who worked indoors, tended to be engaged on fifty-one week contracts, primarily to prevent them claiming poor relief in the parish where employed if dismissed for any reason. Estate maintenance men, woodmen, labourers and others, who were paid weekly or fortnightly, however, had no security of employment of any description and could be sacked immediately if it was considered necessary.

Informal letter of engagement issued in 1889 offering George Hubbard Grass the post of head gamekeeper to the 3rd Earl Manvers at Thoresby Park in Nottinghamshire:

Estates Office,
Thoresby Park,
Newark,
15th March, 1889
Grass,
I am desired by Lord Manvers to say that he will be glad to engage you as head keeper at Thoresby as from 1st. April next, on the following terms: Salary to be £80 a year, £20 per annum for the keep of a cow, 8 tons of coal for the kennels, 1/6d (7½p) per week for all dogs kept by yourself and under-keepers (The number to be settled after you come here.), free house, garden and firewood, and about 7½ acres of grassland – you are also to receive the fees arising from the venison list.

Lord Manvers will provide and keep you a horse and trap for your own use, and also a horse and cart for the deer, as well.

Lord Manvers wishes to adopt the same system as regards pheasant rearing as you have been accustomed to at Eaton, viz 1/6d for all pheasants, being strong healthy birds which have been turned

continued overleaf

into coverts – as to 'Fees' received from gentlemen who shoot at Thoresby, Lord Manvers wishes it to be understood that he reserves the consideration of this matter, but that should he decide not to allow fees, he will make you an allowance not less than £5 per annum in lieu of them – all travelling expenses will of course be refunded to you.

I understand that our present keeper has had to find his own horses, but in future they will be found by his lordship as I have stated, and their keep supplied from the home farm.

A month's notice on either side to terminate the engagement, but it should be understood that except under very exceptional circumstances this will not be given during the shooting season, ie between 1st.Sept. and 1st.Feb.

I shall be glad to receive a line from you accepting these terms and hope that it may be the beginning of an engagement both pleasant and happy for yourself and satisfactory to his lordship.

Personally I can assure you of every support so long as your duties are faithfully and honestly carried out. I have the greatest confidence from what I have heard of you and this will always be the case.

Yours faithfully
W. Wordsworth

Pay

Extract from the wages account for the Broadlands estate in Hampshire listing payments made to the gamekeepers in July 1927. Unusually, the men are paid monthly rather than fortnightly or weekly.

Pay methods for outdoor servants varied somewhat depending upon the estate where they were employed. Generally speaking, though, during the eighteenth and the nineteenth centuries, gamekeepers, gardeners, coachmen and senior hunt servants were paid quarterly, in arrears; live-in staff such as lower grade stables staff and hunt servants, footmen, under-gardeners, dairymaids and some farm workers were paid annually, in arrears; while estate maintenance employees, woodmen, casual farm labourers and seasonally hired itinerant staff were usually paid either weekly or fortnightly. Some landowners continued to operate this payment system until the outbreak of World War One in order to ensure continuity of staff, although by the late Victorian period the great majority had begun to pay all outdoor servants either fortnightly or weekly, whether or not they resided in the servants' quarters or a bothy, or in a cottage on the estate.

Salaries paid to outdoor servants by a 'respectable country gentleman' in 1825, as itemised by Samuel and Sarah Adams in *The Complete Servant*:

> *Head gamekeeper 70 guineas a year, and 13/- per week for board wages; a cottage and firing*
>
> *Under-gamekeeper 1 guinea per week*
>
> *Gardener 40 guineas a year, and 13/- per week for board wages; a house and firing*
>
> *Assistant gardener 12/- per week*
>
> *Coachman 28 guineas a year*
>
> *Groom 12 guineas a year, his liveries and a gratuity*
>
> *Lady's groom 12 guineas a year*
>
> *Dairymaid 8 guineas a year*
>
> *Second dairymaid 7 guineas a year*
>
> *N.B. one guinea equates to £1.05*

Board wages

Board wages were paid to staff who remained at home in the mansion when a landowner and his family were in town for the London season, at their Scottish shooting lodge or travelling abroad for lengthy periods, in order that they could buy their own food and drink instead of being provided with meals in the servants' hall. Coachmen and other stables staff who lived above the stables and dined in the servants' hall were the only outdoor servants who benefited from this supplement, apart from the occasional live-in dairymaid and bachelor chauffeur who resided in the servants' quarters or above the garage. Payments were sometimes quite liberal, enabling servants to save part of the money for a rainy day.

Housing

Every country landowner provided free housing of some description for his outdoor staff. Married men were generally entitled to a house or a cottage, usually with a large garden or a nearby allotment on which to grow vegetables and to keep chickens, a pig and, perhaps a milking cow. Such properties might also be partially or fully furnished, with the rates and tithes (property taxes levied by the Church of England) being paid by the estate. There was no security of tenure, however, and if a man was dismissed because of poor workmanship, bad behaviour or long-term illness, he would invariably be evicted at short notice and have to find accommodation for himself and his family in the local workhouse if he had been unable to find a new situation. Heads of departments lived in specifically designated houses, as befitted their status, often with four or five bedrooms and adjoining accommodation for unmarried staff members and one or two personal servants. It was usual for unmarried gardeners to live in a bothy (hostel) in the gardens, for unmarried farm workers to live in on the home farm, for unmarried stables staff or hunt servants to live in rooms above the stables, for unmarried chauffeurs to live in a flat above the garage or in the servants' quarters at the mansion and for unmarried gamekeepers to live in with the head keeper or in the keepers' bothy. Other unmarried men, in particular locally recruited labourers or tradesmen, either lodged with a colleague or an estate pensioner or lived at home with their parents.

'Model' estate workers cottages at Great Bedwyn, Wiltshire, c1910. Cottages such as these often had staggered entrance doors to give the occupants a certain amount of privacy.

Clothing

Gamekeepers, park keepers, hunt servants, chauffeurs, coachmen, grooms and other 'front of house' stables staff were all provided with free handmade livery uniforms either annually or every two years for use when attending a landowner, his family and guests, when representing a landowner in public, or on special occasions. Such servants were also issued with smart working clothing to be worn when carrying out their day-to-day duties. Some other outdoor servants were supplied with clothing on prestigious estates, too, but this was not the norm. Gardeners, for example, might be issued with matching suits in order to create a good impression in front of visitors, keepers of principal gate lodges might be given a coat and hat or a livery uniform and the boatman might be provided with a livery uniform or a suit. Landowners either had their own customised livery uniforms or tweed suiting, with brass or silver buttons embossed with their coat of arms or cipher on the coat and waistcoat, or used a standard uniform, fitted with their own crested buttons.

Above: A typical Victorian 'model'-style detached estate house with a large garden built to accommodate a senior outdoor servant such as a head gamekeeper or a head forester.

Below: Early twentieth century livery buttons bearing the ciphers of Sir William Waters Butler, Bt. (left), Dr Edward Roberts (centre) and Sir Berkeley Sheffield, Bt. (right).

Farm staff, estate maintenance men, foresters and other outdoor employees, although equally important for the smooth running of a country estate, were not normally provided with free clothing but, nevertheless, were expected to dress in a tidy manner!

Male servants licences

In 1777, the Prime Minister, Lord North introduced a licensing system for male servants that obliged landowners and others to pay an annual fee of one guinea (£1.05) for each manservant employed if they were engaged to undertake a particular role as defined by law. Outdoor servants who required a licence included gardeners, gamekeepers, park keepers, hunt servants, coachmen and stables staff, footmen and others hired in a 'personal, domestic or menial capacity'. Land agents, farm staff, estate yard employees, foresters, lodge keepers and itinerant workers did not have to be licensed. The licence was reduced in price to 15/- (75p) per annum in 1869 but was not finally abolished until 1937 (by which time chauffeurs had been added to the licensing list).

Perks

Outdoor servants benefited from a variety of perquisites, depending upon the department in which they were employed. Gardeners, gamekeepers, coachmen and others who paid regular visits to the mansion as part of their duties were given beer or cider by the butler or one of the footmen and might dine in the servants' hall from time to time. Coal or firewood was usually provided free of charge to gamekeepers, foresters and lodge keepers. Hunt servants were allowed to sell skins from dead farm animals cut up for hound food, and often sold hound manure (which had a high meat content) to tanneries for dyeing purposes. Coachmen were sometimes permitted to sell old coach and carriage wheels for 'pin money'. Departmental heads received gratuities or gifts from tradesmen in return for their business. Gardeners generally had a vegetable allowance. Farm workers were supplied with surplus farm produce as part of their emoluments. Gamekeepers could kill rabbits for the table and were given a 'vermin payment' for every predator that they destroyed. Park keepers had a venison ration and often benefited from the sale of skins of slaughtered deer. On some large estates, every outdoor servant was provided with an annual supply of fuel for firing, a large garden or an allotment for growing vegetables, along with a daily quota of milk from the home farm, and a brace of rabbits, hares or pheasants after a big shoot had taken place.

Advertisement placed in *The Gamekeeper* magazine in 1936 offering to purchase bird wings and small mammal skins. In times past, gamekeepers were usually allowed to sell the skins and feathers as part of their perks. These items were eagerly sought after by furriers, milliners and fishing fly makers.

WANTED for Cash any quantity of :—
Jay Wings ... ... 4d. pair
Crows and Rook Wings ... 1½d. „
Blackbird Wings ... ... 1d. „
Moorhen Wings ... ... 1d. „
Coot Wings... ... ... 1d. „
Highest prices paid for Stoat, Weasel, Mole and Rabbit skins.—The Witton Feather & Skin Co., Stirchley, Birmingham.

Tips

The practice of giving tips or 'vails' to servants appears to date back to the seventeenth century, when it was the custom for visiting dignitaries to distribute small gifts to members of a household where they had been staying. Tipping household staff and certain outdoor servants on a country estate soon became an established tradition, often in return for discreet favours, with some guests handing out generous sums of money. The head gardener could expect to get a cash gratuity for showing a visitor around the gardens and pleasure grounds. Grooms might be given a small sum of money for holding a horse and lodge keepers for opening a gate, while a coachman or a chauffeur would invariably receive a good tip for collecting a guest from a railway station, and an additional payment when he returned him at the end of a visit. The head gamekeeper profited most, though, being paid substantial sums of money by wealthy sporting guests for placing them in the best positions in the shooting line on a driven shoot, and getting a further tip from them at the end of a two- or three-day shooting party. Under-gamekeepers of all grades were generally tipped, too, in recognition of their services at a shoot and were given a gratuity commensurate with their status in the game department.

The Gamekeeper magazine, dated May 1907, included a sample scale of tips paid by sporting guests at Scottish shooting lodges:

Butler £1

First footman 10/-

Chauffeur 10/-

Head keeper (grouse) £1

Second keeper 10/-

Head stalker (deer forest) £3

Second stalker 10/-

Fisherman (ghillie) £1

This is a very moderate estimate. Many head stalkers expect and receive a £5 note if the guest is lucky enough to kill one or two stags.

Legacies

Servants, both outdoor and indoor, often benefited when a landowner died, usually receiving a small cash legacy, a retirement annuity or a valued possession such as a favourite book, a piece of sporting equipment or an ornament of some description. The 1st Duke of Westminster, for example, bequeathed a year's wages to every servant who had been in his employment for more than five years when he died in 1899. Mr Charles Morrison, the millionaire businessman and landowner who passed away in 1909, left a year's wages to each gamekeeper or watcher employed on his various estates in England and Scotland, £1,000 to Mr J.H. Dickson, his land agent on the island of Islay, and £1,000 to Mr William Stanford, his farm bailiff at Basildon Park in Berkshire. Likewise, the 4th Duke of Sutherland, who died in 1913, left £300 to his land agent at Lilleshall in Shropshire, £300 to his land agent at Trentham in Staffordshire and £100 each to his head coachman, his head chauffeur, his head groom and the captain and the engineer of his steam yacht, the *Catania*.

Long-service awards

From the mid-nineteenth century onwards it became something of a tradition for country landowners to present long-serving members of staff with a gift of some description in recognition of their loyalty and contribution to the smooth running of their estate. Some gave inscribed clocks, silver salvers or rose bowls, while others favoured illuminated addresses or purses containing gold or silver or silver coins, the number of coins depending upon the seniority of the recipient. Farm servants of long standing were often eligible for a long-service medal, too, if their employer belonged to the Royal Agricultural Society of England or one of the regional or county agricultural societies.

Travel

Some outdoor servants had the opportunity to travel with their employer as part of their duties. Coachmen and grooms regularly undertook local journeys and, in some households, accompanied the family to London for the season, driving them around town in hired carriages, escorting them when out riding and looking after the horses. Chauffeurs travelled

Long-service clock presented by the 5th Lord Brayebrooke to Robert Feetham, his second keeper at Audley End in Essex, in 1869. The inscription reads *'Presented to Robert Feetham by Charles Cornwallis, Lord Brayebrooke in remembrance of his service as a keeper at Audley End extending over a period of 34 years. April 1869.'*

great distances, particularly during the Edwardian era when it was the custom for wealthy landowners to spend late summer and early autumn shooting, fishing and deer stalking in Scotland and to visit fashionable European spas for health cures. Indeed, prior to outbreak of World War One when border controls on the Continent were virtually non-existent, a chauffeur was expected to be able load a car on to a private yacht, a ferry or a cargo ship safely and to drive his master anywhere in Europe at the drop of a hat if needed. Gamekeepers often travelled, too, accompanying landowners to shooting parties on local or distant estates, or to Scottish sporting properties, either to act as loaders or ghillies. Duncan Macrae, a stalker–keeper employed by the 5th Duke of Sutherland, broke new ground in 1913, sailing to Kenya with his master on a big game hunting expedition in the guise of a professional hunter, while Frank Milton, a gamekeeper with the 2nd Duke of Westminster on the Eaton estate in Cheshire, was seconded to the duke's French estate in Normandy for a couple of seasons in the late 1920s to look after his pack of boar hounds. Staff who travelled either stayed in the servants quarters at their employer's host's house and dined in the servants' hall, lodged in an estate bothy for unmarried men or if visiting London, where town houses were often cramped, were put up in a nearby hotel.

Motor car being loaded on a cross channel ferry at Folkestone 1911. An Edwardian chauffeur was expected to be able to load a car on to a private yacht, ferry or cargo ship safely and to drive his master anywhere in Europe at the drop of a hat.

Healthcare

Staff employed on large country estates owned by the wealthier members of the aristocracy and the landed gentry were generally provided with some kind of healthcare if they had the misfortune to fall ill. The lady of the house or the housekeeper invariably kept a supply of proprietary medicines suitable for common ailments that were dispensed as and when required, both to indoor and outdoor servants. Many landowners paid a retainer to a local doctor so he would attend ill servants. Some also subscribed to a nearby cottage hospital, where treatment could be arranged for anyone with a serious condition. The 11th Duchess of Bedford, who had trained as a nurse, even opened her own cottage hospital on the Woburn Abbey estate in Bedfordshire in 1898, for the benefit of staff and local villagers. Her contemporary, the 6th Duchess of Portland, followed suit, setting up a hospital block at Welbeck Abbey in Nottinghamshire, where ill servants were not only cared for, but kept on full pay throughout their stay. All too often, though, outdoor servants on smaller properties faced the prospect of dismissal and eviction from their home if an illness rendered them unfit to carry out their duties and they frequently ended up in the workhouse along with their families.

Servants' benevolent organisations

In keeping with the Victorian ethos of helping the 'deserving poor', a number of public-spirited individuals set up benevolent organisations during the nineteenth century to provide retirement pensions and accommodation for ageing servants and financial assistance to those who were ill or had fallen on hard times. Some operated solely as charities, while others were modelled along the lines of a friendly society or a contributory pension scheme.

The Servants' Benevolent Institution

Founded in 1846 by a former servant, William Ashwell, the Servants' Benevolent Institution collected subscriptions from wealthy employers in order to provide almshouses and pensions for retired servants, not only from country estates but also from middle-class households in towns and cities. It also made small payments to those who were recovering from an illness. In all cases, applicants had to demonstrate to the governors that they were in genuine need of assistance and of good character!

The Gardeners Royal Benevolent Institution

The Gardeners Royal Benevolent Institution (known as the Gardeners Benevolent Institution until 1851) was formed in 1839 for the purpose of raising money to provide retirement pensions to ageing gardeners employed on country estates and in public gardens in towns and cities. Following the introduction of the state pension in 1909, the organisation gradually shifted its focus from offering pensions to providing retirement accommodation for members of the gardening profession. The institution, renamed as Perennial in 2003, still performs a valuable role at the present time.

The Hunt Servants Benefit Society

Established in 1872 as a friendly society rather than a charity, the main objective of the organisation was to provide a contributory pension scheme for hunt staff to enable them to enjoy a secure retirement. Contributions could either be paid by a hunt servant or by an employer. Funds were kept topped up by regular donations from honorary members and subscribers. The organisation continues to operate today and is now known as the Hunt Staff Benefit Society.

The Keepers' Benefit Society

Effectively an occupational pension scheme funded by members' contributions and donations, the Keepers' Benefit Society was set up in 1886 by Viscount Stormont, Lord Westbury and a number of other influential landowners to provide retirement pensions and sick pay for gamekeepers, and compensation payments to the widows and families of those injured or killed by poachers. Initially successful, with a gamekeeper membership of 786 and 244 honorary subscribers by 1890, the organisation went into a gradual decline following the introduction of the state pension in 1909. The society was finally wound up in 1969, having used its residual funds to purchase retirement annuities for the handful of remaining members.

Keepers' Benefit Society annual rule book and list of honorary subscribers, 1908.

Pensions and sick pay

Prior to the introduction of the state pension in 1909, some of the more affluent landowners provided an old age pension and sick pay for long-serving staff members. The ultra-wealthy 4th Duke of Sutherland, who reigned from 1892 until 1913, not only paid out discretionary pensions and operated a sick pay scheme, but also offered free medical treatment for all the servants on his various estates in England and Scotland, and gave each man one day's paid holiday a year. The 2nd Duke of Westminster personally financed a non-contributory final salary type pension for all his employees on his portfolio of properties in Cheshire, London and Scotland during the first half of the twentieth century. Some industrialists who owned country estates apparently arranged for retired servants to receive a pension from their company pension scheme. Generally speaking, though, it was the custom for a landowner to purchase an annuity for an employee when he retired, thus passing the responsibility for the payment of a pension to the annuity provider.

The Winnings almshouse, Welbeck, Nottinghamshire, c1910. Built by the 6th Duke of Portland during the late Victorian period using prize money from horse racing, the almshouses were originally only available to estate widows but were later offered to widowers and aged couples, too.

Retirement housing

In times past many landowners provided retirement accommodation for long-serving members of staff or their widows, either free of charge or in return for helping out at busy times or undertaking specific duties such as looking after the gate lodge

on a minor driveway, sweeping up around the mansion, beating on a shoot day or chopping firewood. If fortunate, an old retainer might be allowed to continue living in his own cottage, but more usually was allocated a small cottage in an estate village. On some prestigious properties there were even purpose-built almshouses for estate pensioners.

Sir Thomas Acland, Bt., for example, rebuilt the village of Selworthy in the 'model' style in 1828 in order to provide retirement housing for aged and infirm servants and others on the Holnicote estate in Somerset; the 6th Duke of Beaufort maintained an establishment known as the Hospital on the Badminton estate in Gloucestershire in the 1830s, which accommodated fourteen pensioned off men and women on an 'all-found' basis; the 6th Duke of Portland, owner the Welbeck estate in Nottinghamshire from 1879 until 1943, built an almshouse complex at Welbeck for retired staff during the late Victorian period using the proceeds from his horse racing activities, which he named, appropriately, The Winnings. If an aged unmarried pensioner or a widower was having difficulty coping on his own, it was the custom on some estates for him to be given lodgings with an employee and his family, his living expenses being paid by the landowner.

The end of the day

Outdoor servants of long standing on a large country estate owned by a leading member of the aristocracy or the landed gentry usually enjoyed a comfortable retirement, not only receiving a pension or an annuity and free accommodation of some description, but also an annual Christmas box and, perhaps, the occasional brace of rabbits, hares of game birds for the pot during the shooting season. Many derived a small income from their savings, too, having accrued a nest egg by banking part of their wages, their tips and their gratuities from tradesmen over the years. Further, some landowners or their wives made a point of visiting old retainers from time to time to see that all was well. Captain T.P. Lewes, for example, owner of the Llanayron estate in Cardiganshire from 1919 to 1940, regularly rode out in his pony and trap to see pensioners or their widows, always taking them a bottle of port from his cellar for 'medicinal' purposes! Similarly, during the first half of the twentieth century, the 9th Duchess of Devonshire called on the sick and elderly whenever she stayed on her husband's various estates in England and Ireland. Employers of this calibre invariably attended the funeral of any former head of department or of a servant who had spent a lifetime 'in the family' or sent a representative in their place, and might also pay for a suitably inscribed headstone for his grave.

Servant's headstone in Wimborne St Giles Churchyard, Dorset. The inscription reads 'Thomas Warner, gardiner to the Lord Ashley's father and grandfather. Skillful in his place, industrial, honest, faithful, he lived in the faith. Died Feb.1657'.

Sadly, many outdoor servants were either obliged to apply for outdoor poor relief from the local Board of Guardians or for financial assistance from one of the servants' benevolent organisations (where applicable) in order to survive after they had become incapable of working any longer, or to seek refuge with their children or suffer the indignity of ending their days in the nearest workhouse and being buried in a pauper's grave. Such servants often ended up in this situation simply because of working on a succession of different estates during the course of their lifetime, by being employed on a small estate or by a landowner who had fallen on hard times, or through dismissal due to illness or misconduct. 🪶

Above: Cambrook House, the Clutton Union Workhouse at Temple Cloud in Somerset, c1910. Built in 1837 for the Clutton Board of Guardians, it housed around 140 inmates who came from a large group of rural parishes, many of whom were aged or infirm outdoor servants, farm labourers or their widows.

Right: James Pitt Dury, Master of the Clutton Union Workhouse from 1856 until his death in 1892. The grandson of a coachman whose widow died in Chertsey Workhouse in Surrey in 1849, he had a reputation for treating his charges in a firm but fair manner and did as much as possible to help able-bodied inmates get back into work and provide decent surroundings for the old and the sick.

18

THE COUNTRY ESTATE
AT PLAY

LIFE WAS NOT all hard work and no play for the outdoor servant on a country estate in times past, notwithstanding the fact that many worked a twelve- or fourteen-hour day, six and a half days a week with little time to devote to leisure activities apart from church or chapel attendance on a Sunday. Indeed, from the mid-nineteenth century onwards many landowners started to provide sports and social activities for their staff, to organise Christmas parties and occasional servants' balls, to put on celebratory meals and dances to commemorate family or royal events, or to give employees time off to attend local fetes, fairs or agricultural shows. Some also began to allow senior staff members, both indoor and outdoor, to use their private golf course, to ride to hounds or to fish on estate waters during their spare time, or offered other privileges within their gift.

The gardeners at The Warren, Hayes, Kent, enjoying a smoke, a drink and a game of cards outside the gardeners' bothy (hostel) on their afternoon off, 1912,

Servants balls, christmas festivities and celebrations

The annual servants' ball was undoubtedly one of the highlights of the staff calendar on every country estate, either large or small. Generally held early in the New Year after the household festivities had concluded, it was hosted by the landowner and his wife, who invariably danced with members of the assembled company, and took place in a large room in the mansion, rarely if ever visited by outdoor employees. Each servant was expected to dress for the occasion in their best clothing and was allowed to bring one guest who, if male, had to be a relative or an acceptable suitor. It was usual for a meal of some kind to be provided, either a buffet or a sit down meal consisting of several courses, accompanied, of course, by beer or wine.

On some estates, the servants' ball was a very grand occasion indeed, where no expense was spared. At Welbeck Abbey in Nottinghamshire, for example, the 6th Duke of Portland, who employed more than 250 indoor and outdoor staff, hired a London orchestra to play dance music and a team of fifty waiters to attend to the needs of his guests. At Longleat in Wiltshire, an equally opulent establishment, both servants and local tradesmen were invited to the ball, which was held in the dining room. The host, the 5th Marquess of Bath, always opened the floor with the housekeeper, while the Marchioness danced with the house steward. Other heads of departments followed suit with female members of the Bath family. On the Rufford Abbey estate in Nottinghamshire, the servants' ball, somewhat unusually, took place on New Year's Eve in the old crypt of the abbey at the same time as the owner, the 2nd Lord Saville hosted a glittering ball upstairs for a large complement of high society guests. Lord and Lady Saville did not neglect their employees, though, and always found the time to leave their own ball for half an hour or so during the course of the evening to wish everyone a happy new year, and to partner a few favoured individuals for a dance or two!

Christmas was a particularly important event on a country estate during the late Victorian and the Edwardian periods. Staff would be invited into the great hall of the mansion and given a useful present off the tree or from a heavily loaded trestle table. The estate children would be entertained at a lavish party hosted by the lady of the house and supervised by the butler, and they were presented with a gift as they left. At Sandbeck Park in Yorkshire the 10th Earl of Scarborough and his countess had a fat beast slaughtered and gave every outdoor employee a joint of beef (allowing 2lb for each adult and 1lb for every child) for their Christmas dinner on the Saturday before Christmas, together with several loaves of bread. They also handed out clothing and bedding to each family at the annual Workmen's Ball held during the Christmas period. On Brownsea in Poole Harbour in Dorset, the owner, Charles Van Raalte, entertained his outdoor servants and their families to a sumptuous luncheon of roast pheasant and chicken in Brownsea Castle on Christmas Day, after which presents from the Christmas tree were distributed to the children. Everyone stayed on for a festive dinner, with copious amounts of mulled wine and cider on hand, which finished at around 10 p.m.. At Kingston Lacey in Dorset, the chatelaine, Mrs Henrietta Bankes, who did not provide a servants' ball or children's party at Christmas, nevertheless put on a roast beef Christmas dinner for her staff. She also gave each woman a length of cloth for dressmaking and a box of chocolates and each man 10/- (50p) and a box (present) or a bottle of port. The only seasonal gesture that Boer War hero, the 4th Lord Vivian made, however, was to dress up as a Chinaman on Christmas Day and invite his estate workers into his country house at Glynn in Cornwall during the afternoon to collect a present from a special servants' Christmas Tree, giving each man a short lecture about unsatisfactory work and 'not putting your shoulder to the wheel' as he received his gift!

Servants ball at Rushmore Lodge – Victorian style

Staff festivities were normally very private affairs and not generally discussed by all and sundry. That said, the 4th Lord Rivers allowed the *Salisbury Journal* to carry the following report about the annual ball held for servants and others connected with the Rushmore estate in Wiltshire in December 1858:

Lord and Lady Rivers gave their annual ball for servants and their friends, tenants and tradesmen at Rushmore Lodge on Friday, 31st. December. This affair has become notorious, as one of the very best things of the kind in England and, while it reflects the greatest honour upon this truly English nobleman and his lady, for the generous and openhearted way in which they treat those under them, it also reflects great credit upon those who have the management, as well as those who partake of this annual treat. The dancing took place in the noble dining saloon, an orchestra being erected for the accommodation of Mr Eyers and his very excellent Quadrille Band. Dancing commenced at half-past seven, and was kept up until nearly six the next morning, the company being honoured; the whole of the evening, by the presence of Lord and Lady Rivers and family, and several other distinguished visitors, who joined in all the dances, and appeared to derive as much enjoyment as anyone present. Refreshments, of every possible

continued overleaf

description, were most profusely supplied during the whole of the evening. The supper, which took place around one o'clock, was on a magnificent scale, and consisted of dishes of every possible kind, from the most substantial rounds of beef, and ornamented boar's heads, down to the choicest delicacy, every dish beautifully ornamented, and the tables highly decorated with flowers, &c. It need not be said that full justice was done to this noble repast. It gives us great pleasure to record that, while everything was provided on the most unbounded scale of liberality, no one out stepped the bounds of moderation, but all met, enjoyed themselves to their heart's content, and parted as rational beings ought to do.

Rushmore Lodge c1910.

Country landowners often organised events for their employees to celebrate coronations, royal jubilees, family weddings, twenty-first birthdays and similar occasions. The 3rd Earl Manvers not only held a luncheon party for his departmental heads and estate workmen and their wives at Thoresby Park in Nottinghamshire on 22 June 1897 to commemorate Queen Victoria's Diamond Jubilee, but also opened his gardens and pleasure grounds for their benefit in the afternoon, put on a substantial tea for the estate children at which a medal and a mug was presented to each child, and hosted a dance in the evening that finished at midnight. To celebrate

SHERBORNE CASTLE   SEP. 5TH, 1906.

his eldest son's twenty-first birthday in 1909, the 4th Duke of Sutherland put on staff dinners and dances, ox roasts and children's parties on all of his English and Scottish estates. The event at his ancestral home, Dunrobin Castle in Sutherland, took place over several days with a firework display, a sports gathering and illuminations from two battleships anchored off the nearby port of Golspie. In January 1861 the 4th Lord Rivers, known for his generosity, hosted a lavish supper followed by dancing for his servants at Rushmore Lodge in Wiltshire to mark the marriage of his daughter, the Honourable Fanny Pitt, to the Marquess of Carmarthen and gave each labourer on the estate 10/- (50p) (the equivalent of a week's wages) to provide a good meal for himself and his family in his own home to celebrate the occasion. In addition to throwing a staff party, the 1st Lord Illingworth also invited his head gamekeeper, George Grass, and other key employees to attend his wedding and the reception afterwards as personal guests when he married Miss Margaret Wilberforce at Bishop Thornton in Yorkshire in 1931. Some employers even allowed a senior member of staff or a servant of long standing to use a room in their mansion for the wedding reception of a son or daughter and provided suitable food, drink and musical entertainment for the assembled company!

Bunting hung on poles along the main driveway to Sherborne Castle in Dorset to celebrate the twenty-first birthday of the owner, Frederick Wingfield Digby, 1906. The banner attached to the top of the decorated archway reads 'Long Live The Squire'.

The estate cricket team

Cricketing enthusiasts among the landowning fraternity inevitably had their own estate cricket team consisting of family members and indoor and outdoor servants, who practised together on an equal footing and played against local village and estate teams. The 6th Duke of Portland, who formed an estate cricket club at Welbeck Abbey in Nottinghamshire in 1884, was one of a number of employers to provide his team with a ground and a pavilion. Two of his staff players, Daniel Bottom, a forester, and Edward Alletson, a carpenter, later became county cricketers, the former for Derbyshire and Nottinghamshire, the latter for Nottinghamshire. The 2nd Duke of Westminster, an enthusiastic all-round sportsman who also ran his own football team, not only bankrolled an estate cricket club at Eaton Hall in Cheshire, enlisting estate workers, tenant farmers and local retired Army officers to play for him but also engaged a full-time professional, Jack I'Anson, a former county cricketer who played for Lancashire, to coach his men. Lord Newton, owner of the Lyme Park estate in Cheshire between 1898 and 1942, apparently selected outdoor staff who could play cricket in preference to non-cricketers. It goes without saying, of course, that some over-zealous head gamekeepers objected to cricketing under-keepers being engaged on estates on the basis that they could not carry out their duties effectively during the pheasant rearing season.

Above: Boys' cricket team on a country estate c1870.

Right: The pavilion for the estate cricket team at Hackwood Park in Hampshire. Founded during the late Victorian period by Walter Raynbird, a son of Lord Bolton's land agent (and later the land agent himself) at Hackwood, the club was originally set up for the benefit of estate employees who played cricket against local village teams and other estate teams.

Sir Edward Hulse's birthday cricket match

The annual cricket match between married and single men took place on Friday, 31 August, which was Sir Edward Hulse's birthday. The employees on the Breamore estate were given a half-holiday and provided with refreshments. A good number of spectators were present at the cricket match, and during the afternoon selections of music were played by the Fordingbridge Volunteer and Town Band. For the married, E.D. Stanford batted well for 49, while for the single, R. Latimer and C.H. Stanford were responsible for 57 and 16 respectively. Amongst those present at the match were the Hon. Lady Hulse, the Dowager Lady Hulse, Miss Goff, the Hon. Mrs Foley, Mrs Snow, the Misses Dew, &c. After tea, which was served in the cricket pavilion, the Rev. E.J. Latimer, in a few well chosen words, congratulated Sir E. Hulse on having attained his seventeenth birthday: and Sir Edward, in reply, said he hoped to celebrate many more birthdays in a similar manner. After a good game, the single men won by 15 runs on the first innings.

The Salisbury Journal, 8 September 1906

The estate social club

During the Edwardian era, a number of more enlightened employers established social clubs for the benefit of their staff members, often with a small lending library of specially selected literature and magazines. The 4th Duke of Sutherland opened a 'Club Room and Institute for Servants and Workmen' in a building in the back stable yard at Lilleshall Hall in Shropshire, providing leisure and elementary educational facilities for members. Mrs Ronnie Greville, the well-known society hostess, ran a social club in the servants' quarters at Polesden Lacey in Surrey for her staff every Friday evening with a bar, music and a billiards table. The 5th Marquess of Bath organised social evenings in the servants' hall at Longleat in Wiltshire for his employees twice weekly on Tuesdays and Thursdays, hiring a pianist from the nearby town of Warminster to play dance music and putting on a generous buffet supper produced by the kitchen and stillroom staff – the housekeeper, of course kept an eagle eye on the young maids to ensure that they did not become too familiar with the unmarried grooms and gardeners from the bothy! Lord Louis Mountbatten (later Earl Mountbatten of Burma), however, broke new ground in his estate club at Adsdean in Sussex in the early 1930s, installing a radio set, then something of a luxury even among the upper classes, and arranging film shows for his servants on a regular basis, in addition to purchasing a billiards table, dart board and a range of other games.

Lord Louis Mountbatten (pictured here with Lady Mountbatten in the mid-1920s) broke new ground at his estate club at Adsdean in the early 1930s, not only installing a radio set but also organising staff film shows on a regular basis.

The estate band

Some landowners with a musical bent ran their own estate band, not only to entertain guests but also to play at village fetes and other local functions. The well-known archaeologist, General Augustus Pitt-Rivers, formed a band on the Rushmore estate in Wiltshire during the late Victorian period specifically 'to broaden the interests of the villagers and to enliven the Sabbath'. He recruited estate workers and others as bandsmen, provided them with a uniform based upon that of a keeper on Cranborne Chase and enlisted the help of Dan Godfrey, bandmaster of his old regiment, the Grenadier Guards, to train them as musicians. Charles Van Raalte, owner of Brownsea Island in Poole Harbour from 1901 until 1908 made it a condition of employment that estate workers, whatever their particular skills, should be able to play an instrument in the Brownsea Island Estate Band, which performed both at Brownsea Castle and at political and social events in Poole and the surrounding districts under the direction of Mr Campbell, the estate carpenter, who doubled as bandmaster. 'Squire' Maude Cheape, chatelaine of the Bentley estate in Worcestershire, in stark contrast, conscripted stable and kennel staff who could play the piano, violin and other instruments into a makeshift band to play jazz and other music for the benefit of her family, guests and non-musical employees whenever she visited her hunting and shooting box at Haselor in Warwickshire in the 1890s.

The Motcombe Estate scout troop

If a landowner or his wife set up a branch of a national organisation of any kind for the benefit of the local community, it was usual for senior servants to be encouraged to get involved either as office bearers or as participants during their limited spare time. For example, when Lady Stalbridge established a scout troop for the sons of staff and tenants on the Motcombe estate

in Dorset in 1914, she became president and appointed David Farmer, the electrician at Motcombe House, as scout master and Mrs Bourne, wife of the head gardener, as cub mistress, while her son, the Honourable Hugh Grosvenor, enrolled as a boy scout along with the village lads. Every year, before the scouts went off to summer camp, she asked the Motcombe tenant farmers to give older boys in their employment permission to attend. The troop was disbanded shortly after Lord Stalbridge sold the estate in 1925 and he and Lady Stalbridge left the area.

Boy scout c1914.

The hunt

On country estates that had their own hunt establishment or where hunting took place on a regular basis, it was not unusual for outdoor staff to be invited along as spectators if a meet of hounds or harriers took place on the property. They would, of course, be expected to stand a discreet distance away from the pack and the mounted field, but would invariably be provided with sandwiches and alcoholic refreshment in a nearby outbuilding or barn. Both the 10th Earl of Scarborough at Sandbeck Park in Yorkshire and Algernon Heber-Percy at Hodnet Hall in Shropshire arranged for the local school to be closed on the morning of a hunt in order that the estate children could attend such meets. Some hunting orientated landowners with small private packs of hounds or harriers occasionally allowed senior outdoor servants who could ride a horse to follow the hounds on a weekday meet, lending them a mount for the purpose. Others, particularly those holding the mastership of a well-known pack of hounds, insisted that their head gamekeeper joined the field on a specially supplied hunter whenever the hunt met in the vicinity of their estate so as to give advice to the huntsmen on where a fox could be found and to prevent any conflict of interest between game preservation and fox hunting.

The Brocklesby Foxhounds in front of Brocklesby Park, Lincolnshire, 1910. Outdoor staff were often invited along as spectators and provided with suitable refreshments whenever a meet of hounds or harriers took place on a country estate.

Staff privileges

Senior staff members on large, prestigious estates owned by benevolent landowners often enjoyed a number of privileges not normally bestowed upon persons of their class. Upper servants employed by the 6th Duke of Portland at Welbeck Abbey in Nottinghamshire, by the 1st Earl of Iveagh on the Elveden estate in Suffolk and by the 2nd Duke of Westminster at Eaton Hall in Cheshire were allowed to play golf on the private golf course. Staff at Llanayron in Cardiganshire had permission to fish for salmon and sea trout on the river Aeron. Gamekeepers in the service of the 15th Earl of Pembroke at Wilton House in Wiltshire were given free passes and time off to attend race meetings at Salisbury racecourse. Estate workers on Brownsea Island in Poole Harbour in Dorset during the Edwardian era were offered a day's deer stalking each November in order that they could obtain venison for the table at Christmastime. Head gardeners on certain properties were permitted to take friends and local dignities on garden tours during periods when their employer and his family were not in residence, while head gamekeepers might be allowed to put on a rabbit shoot for colleagues from other departments or tenant farmers, or invite them out for a day's ferreting.

Fairs and fetes

Outdoor servants were occasionally given time off to
attend local fairs, fetes or similar events, particularly if
relevant to their trade or if organised by an employer in
aid of a church or charity. Shepherds would invariably
attend any sheep fair in the vicinity with the bailiff
from the estate home farm in order to buy and sell
sheep and lambs. Ploughmen, carters, dairymen,
labourers and other farm staff on annual contracts who

were in search of promotion or unhappy with their lot travelled to an autumn 'hiring
fair', usually held either on Michaelmas Day (29 September) or Martinmas Day (11
November), to seek a new position, carrying all their worldly goods in a small bag
or suitcase. The head groom, the head gardener and the farm bailiff on a large estate
might exhibit livestock, flowers and produce at a nearby show or be invited to act as
a judge in the relevant classes. On the Normanby estate in Lincolnshire, the owner,
Sir Berkeley Sheffield, Bt., formed an agricultural and horticultural society in 1884
for the benefit of tenants and employees, which held an annual show for livestock,
flowers and garden produce in the grounds of the mansion until the outbreak of
World War One; while at Welbeck Abbey in Nottinghamshire the Welbeck Tenants'
Agricultural Society put on a show every year specifically for horses, cattle, sheep and
poultry and awarded prizes for the best cultivated farms on the property.

Above: Gamekeepers and
farmers posing for the
camera with the day's bag
on a rabbit shoot c1900.
The right to organise a
rabbit shoot for colleagues
and tenant farmers was
a perk enjoyed by some
head gamekeepers.

Left: East Harling Sheep
Fair, Norfolk, 1899. Estate
shepherds regularly
attended local sheep fairs
with the bailiff of the home
farm to buy and sell sheep
and lambs.

19

THE COUNTRY ESTATE IN WARTIME

GARDENERS, GAMEKEEPERS, FARM labourers, chauffeurs, grooms and other country estate staff played a crucial role in defending Great Britain both in World War One and in World War Two, either on active service overseas or on the home front. The 'service to the nation' tradition of estate employees, however, dates back to the early nineteenth century when landowners encouraged their men to join 'home defence' battalions of local regiments, which had been raised to counteract a possible French invasion. Later, during the Victorian period it was not uncommon for employers with a military background to allow men to enlist in the county militia or yeomanry regiment, giving them time off to attend the annual camp, and lending them a horse if they were attached to the cavalry. Some estates even had their own troop or platoon in the county regiment at this time, consisting entirely of male staff members.

Following the declaration of the Boer War in 1899, many estate employees serving as part-time soldiers in the militia or yeomanry sailed for South Africa to fight alongside members of the regular Army. Of those who returned home safely at the end of the conflict in 1902, a number remained in the territorial forces and served their country once again during World War One.

World War One

The outbreak of World War One signalled the death knell for the country estate, a centuries' old institution managed by benevolent landowners who provided employment for generations of estate workers, who used traditional rural skills to maintain farms and livestock, woods and forests, game preserves, gardens and park land and historic stately homes in an environmentally sensitive manner. Some 400,000 male estate employees, both outdoor and indoor, went off to war, many of whom died on the battlefield or left private service forever following the cessation of hostilities in 1918. Three million acres of grassland were ploughed up to increase supplies of home-produced food. Forests and woods were decimated to provide timber for use

Opposite: Nurses with recuperating servicemen outside Temple Newsam House near Leeds – one of the many country houses turned into a wartime convalescent home.

in the war effort. Thousands of acres of land were requisitioned for Army camps and battlefield training grounds, for prisoner of war camps, for airfields and for munitions factories. Game preservation activities were scaled down dramatically, while stocks of game birds and herds of deer were culled for food purposes or poached for 'the pot'. Country houses were turned into hospitals and convalescent homes and the gardens either given over to vegetable growing or abandoned in their entirety due to staff shortages. Farm workers, gamekeepers, gardeners, chauffeurs, grooms and other estate staff were replaced for the duration by breech-clad land girls, conscientious objectors, Belgian refugees, German prisoners of war and daughters of the aristocracy and the gentry who found it something of a novelty to 'get their hands dirty' for the first time in their life!

Enlistment schemes

Patriotic landowners throughout the country encouraged their estate workers to enlist in the armed services, sometimes offering incentives to their men to go to war. The Earl of Durham, Lord Leconfield and the Earl of Lonsdale dismissed all men of military age but guaranteed to keep their jobs open if they joined the Army. The Marquess of Lincolnshire allowed dependants of employees who had joined up to remain in their cottages rent-free for the duration of the conflict. The Earl of Ancaster, not only kept jobs open for estate staff who volunteered to fight for their country and paid them a bonus of £5, but also provided a guaranteed income for their wives and families and allowed them to remain in their homes free of charge.

Some landowners inevitably tried to retain key estate employees of military age, designating gardeners, gamekeepers, stables staff and others as 'farm workers' in order that they could continue to enjoy a relatively normal country lifestyle in wartime. In an effort to persuade these individuals to follow the example of their peers, in January 1915, *Country Life* asked:

1) Have you a Butler, Groom, Chauffeur, Gardener or Gamekeeper serving you who, at this moment should be serving your King and Country?
2) Have you a man serving at your table who should be serving at a gun?
3) Have you a man digging your garden who should be digging trenches?
4) Have you a man driving your car who should be driving a transport wagon?
5) Have you a man preserving your game who should be helping to preserve your Country?

A great responsibility rests on you. Will you sacrifice your personal convenience for your Country's need. Ask your men to enlist TO-DAY.

Opposite (top): William Grass, foreman gardener to Sir Robert Laidlaw at The Warren, Hayes, Kent, who served as a private soldier in the King's Royal Rifle Corps during World War One. Badly gassed on the battlefield in France, he suffered from ill health for the rest of his life and died at the relatively early age of forty-six in 1932.

Opposite (bottom): In addition to driving cars, some chauffeurs became dispatch riders in the Royal Engineers Signal Service (such as the soldier pictured above on a Douglas motorcycle) due to their superlative road navigation skills.

By the time conscription was introduced in 1916, making it compulsory for all able-bodied men aged between eighteen and forty-one to enlist in the armed forces, virtually all the estate employees who had remained in their jobs had joined up, some of whom were well above military age. Other than chauffeurs, gamekeepers and hunt servants who were deployed in a number specialist regiments or corps, estate workers generally served in their local county regiment, in their employer's family regiment, with a rifle brigade or in the Royal Navy, if based in a coastal area.

Chauffeurs

Chauffeurs and chauffeur–mechanics were highly sought after by the armed services in World War One for their driving and engineering skills. Some joined the Army Service Corps (renamed the Royal Army Service Corps in 1917) and either drove senior officers around in staff cars, both at home and abroad, or became lorry drivers in France, transporting supplies to keep convoys moving. Others were recruited by the Royal Army Medical Corps as ambulance drivers, removing casualties from the battlefield to field hospitals or ambulance trains. Those with a good mechanical knowledge were often drafted into the Royal Engineers to service military vehicles.

In some instances, a chauffeur remained with his employer as an officer's 'batman' or personal driver. George Powell, for example, chauffeur to the 2nd Duke of Westminster, served with the duke in an armoured car squadron of the Royal Naval Air Service throughout the war years, driving a succession of Rolls-Royces that had been converted into armoured vehicles. He even received the Distinguished Conduct Medal in 1916 after accompanying the duke on a successful mission to rescue the survivors of a naval vessel being held by Turkish soldiers in the Libyan Desert.

On the home front, wartime driving duties on country estates were carried out by women, boys who had just left school and elderly coachmen, gamekeepers, valets, butlers and others who had learned to drive a car. Exceptionally, a landowner who

acted as a local recruiting officer, served as a magistrate or was engaged in essential work of national importance managed to retain his chauffeur, but this was not encouraged by the authorities.

Hunt servants

Like chauffeurs, hunt servants were much in demand in the Army during World War One for their expertise with horses. Many younger men enlisted as soldiers in cavalry regiments or became horse servants (Army grooms) to officers, while those who were older or more experienced either joined the Army Veterinary Corps or the Army Remount Service, the organisation responsible for sourcing and supplying horses and mules to all Army units. Some hunts lost two or three men. The Portman Hunt in Dorset, under the mastership of the octogenarian 2nd Viscount Portman, for example was deprived of both whippers-in and the second horseman.

Hunting continued to be carried out on a more or less normal scale in many areas for the duration of the war by elderly masters of hounds or committees of volunteers, although some packs reduced the numbers of hounds or harriers kept. Hunt servants who had join up were generally replaced by retired huntsmen, 'gentlemen' huntsmen of above military age, female or teenage whippers-in and school leavers who acted as kennelmen.

Hunting in wartime

Reporting on the current status of hunting in the 1916–17 edition of *Baily's Hunting Directory*, the editor informed readers:

> *Masters of hounds and hunting folk generally have willingly surrendered their staffs, and with a few exceptions, all the Hunt servants and all the grooms of military age are now with the Colours. This, as can be readily understood, means that the many kennels and stables of the Hunts, and of individual hunting people, have to depend upon veterans and boys who have not reached military age. Nor is the supply of veteran hunt servants and grooms a large one. It has, however been discovered that a pack of hounds can get through the work in the field under the charge of a huntsman and one good whipper-in, and last winter, I who write, not only saw good sport with packs so managed, but I also saw a pack at work with a single man in scarlet (a kennel huntsman) and he was whipped-in to by the two daughters of the Master. Of the financial side of the question it need only be said that sufficient money is being found somehow for the 'carrying on' of the Hunts. The more affluent Masters have done wonders in this respect, and though many of the rank and file of hunting men and women have been hard hit by the war, there appears to be, or there really is a general resolve that no Hunt shall be allowed to disappear.*

Opposite (top): Staff on a Pembrokeshire estate c1915. Much reduced in size due to the enlistment of the younger men, the gardener and the chauffeur were the only remaining males and in addition to carrying out their normal duties were expected to turn their hand to a multitude of other tasks. The semi-uniform jacket and the cap badge worn by the chauffeur indicate that he belongs to one of the wartime home defence organisations.

Opposite (bottom): Sidney Tucker, huntsman of the Devon & Somerset staghounds, one of a number of huntsmen of above military age who kept packs of hounds going during World War One.

Gamekeepers

In the region of 23,000 gamekeepers were employed on sporting estates throughout England, Wales, Scotland and Ireland when Great Britain declared war on Germany in August 1914. Experienced with gun and rifle and possessing a multitude of fieldcraft skills, keepers, both young and old, flocked to enlist in the armed services to fight for their country, encouraged by employers and the shooting press. Those already serving in local territorial units were sent to the front straightaway, often being transferred to rifle regiments as snipers, while men from coastal estates who were Naval Reservists were sent to sea as ships' gunners. Inexperienced keepers were trained up as soldiers but were usually deployed on ordinary fighting duties by officers who did not appreciate their capabilities! In certain circumstances, a keeper–soldier might be even excused from general service and appointed an officer's batman or driver.

Henry Clayton Grass (on right), an under-keeper employed by the Earl of Durham on the Lambton Castle estate in Co. Durham. He enlisted as a private soldier in the Durham Light Infantry shortly after the outbreak of World War One in 1914 and was killed in action in France on 26 May 1918 aged twenty-eight. His widow, Jane, was provided with a free house for life and a small pension by the Earl of Durham, and given support to bring up their infant daughter, Irene.

Some gamekeepers managed to transfer to specialist units such as the Lovat Scouts, the Scottish keepers and stalkers regiment, or the 1st Sportsman's Battalion of the Royal Fusiliers, where their skills were put to good use. Later in the war, suitable openings were found for keepers in the Lovat Scouts (Sharpshooters) unit, formed in 1916, and the Army Messenger Dog Service, established in 1917, which trained and worked dogs that were used to track and find wounded men on the battlefield or to carry dispatches and small packages between the lines.

Scores of gamekeepers were wounded in the various theatres of war or suffered from the debilitating effects of gas exposure while in the trenches. The more serious casualties, which could not be dealt with a field ambulance stations, were sent back to England for treatment at military hospitals or country houses that had been converted into temporary convalescent homes. Many keepers were left physically or mentally scarred for life. Bert Tiller, an under-keeper at Broadlands in Hampshire and a private in the Wiltshire Regiment, had his right arm permanently damaged by shell fire and spent two years in hospital recuperating from this and other injuries. Private Cyril Ford, a Dorset keeper, was temporarily blinded by mustard gas and was to suffer permanently from catarrh and a nervous twitch for the rest of his days. Private Peter Eggleton of the Middlesex Regiment, a beat keeper at Six Mile Bottom in Cambridgeshire, sustained severe head injuries at Ypres. He was recovered from the battlefield several days after the end of the battle, had a plate permanently fitted to his skull and suffered from severe headaches thereafter.

In addition to the gamekeepers who were wounded on the battlefield, a number of keepers were taken prisoner by the enemy and sent to prisoner of war camps in Germany and elsewhere. Some were lucky enough to be posted to farms, where they worked under the supervision of armed guards and were reasonably well fed; others were made to work in factories in appalling conditions. Private Frederick Bushell, for example, a Berkshire keeper who was captured at the start of the Battle of the Somme in June 1916, spent three years at a camp in Westphalia where he experienced many hardships working in an iron foundry, often being forced to do twenty-four hour shifts.

Gamekeepers did their bit for the war effort on the home front, too, either combining their duties with farm and forestry work, becoming involved in training or home defence activities in their spare time, or taking on a completely different job for the duration of the war. George Grass, head keeper to Lord Knaresborough at Marton-cum-Grafton in Yorkshire, was instrumental in establishing a branch of the Volunteer Training Corps, a home defence organisation formed to protect the country in the event of an enemy invasion. Roderick Mackenzie, stalker-keeper at Hamnavay on the remote west coast of the island of Lewis in the Outer Hebrides, became a part-time Royal Navy watcher and patrolled the local coastline twice daily, keeping a lookout for any enemy shipping movements in the area and making regular reports from his house to HMS *Iolaire* in Stornoway via a specially installed telegraph line. Mr W. Derrick, head keeper to Lord Crawshaw at Long Whatton in Leicestershire, joined the staff of a munitions factory as an assistant, rose to the position of works manager and was awarded the OBE for putting out a fire that averted a serious explosion.

Elsie Reeves, who worked as an under-keeper on the Whatcombe estate in Dorset during World War One while several of the male gamekeepers were away in the armed services fighting for their country.

Women assisted the gamekeepers in their work on a number of estates, preserving pheasants and partridges, trapping vermin and acting as beaters on shoot days. In several instances, where a single-handed keeper had gone to war, his wife kept things going with the help of her children. Full-time female gamekeepers were employed by landowners, too, to make up for the shortfall in men. Lord Montagu of Beaulieu engaged Miss Hilary Dent as a keeper at Beaulieu in Hampshire, but stipulated that she 'was not allowed to go out on night duty unaccompanied'. Mr Mansel-Pleydell appointed Elsie Reeves as an under-keeper on the Whatcombe estate in Dorset. Indeed, the growing popularity of female keepers at this time prompted the Carreras Ltd., manufacturers of Black Cat cigarettes, to feature one on a cigarette card in its 'Women on War Work' series.

Private Percy Grass of the Suffolk Regiment, a gamekeeper on the Six Mile Bottom estate in Cambridgeshire, who was killed in action in France in 1917. *Courtesy of W.G. Barton.*

Many gamekeepers were decorated for bravery on the battlefield during World War One. Sergeant Adam Gordon of the Yorkshire Hussars, gamekeeper to Lord Helmsley, was awarded the Military Medal and the Distinguished Conduct Medal for his work as a sniper. Private Denis O'Brien of the Irish Guards, a member of the gamekeeping staff at Cahir Park in Co. Tipperary, not only received the Military Medal but was also presented with the Croix de Guerre by the Belgian government for his services at the Battle of Boesinghe. Lovat Scout, Corporal Duncan Macrae, a keeper–stalker at Eishken on the Isle of Lewis, secured the Military Medal for 'Great gallantry and coolness under shell fire' while serving in France.

Sadly, quite a number of gamekeepers were to make the supreme sacrifice for their country during the course of the war, being killed in action on the battlefields of Europe or on the high seas, or dying of their wounds in a military hospital. The Sandringham estate alone lost nine keepers between 1914 and 1918. Three out of the four keepers from the Wentworth Woodhouse estate in Yorkshire that went to war were killed in action. Two keepers from the Lambton Castle estate in Co. Durham died on the battlefield in France. The Buriton estate in Hampshire, the Scaliscro estate on the Isle of Lewis and the Six Mile Bottom estate in Cambridgeshire all lost a keeper apiece. And so the list goes on …

Estate workers' contribution to the war effort

Estate workers made a valuable contribution to the war effort, both in the armed services and on the home front in the Volunteer Training Corps, where men of above military age or exempted from the services for various reasons carried out guard duties on railway lines, canals and reservoirs in strategic locations, attended agricultural camps or undertook other essential defence-related duties. A surprising number received decorations for bravery for their heroic action on the battlefield or at sea. Private William Holmes of the Grenadier Guards, formerly a groom on the Stanway estate in Gloucestershire, was posthumously awarded the Victoria Cross for 'Most conspicuous bravery and devotion to duty' at Cattienières in France in 1918. Captain E.W. Hayward of the Tank Corps, a head chauffeur in civilian life, received the Distinguished Conduct Medal for his services driving a tank in the face of enemy fire in France in 1917. Sergeant Charles Grass of the 19th Corps of the 35th Division, a bricklayer in the Duke of Rutland's building department at Belvoir Castle in Leicestershire, won the Military Medal for leading a 'subsection of Vickers guns with splendid dash and courage' near Zandvoorde in Belgium in 1918.

Country estates lost some of their finest men during World War One. They were not only killed in action but were also severely injured and unable to return to their former jobs. Having seen something of the world during their time in the armed forces, many workers forsook private service forever, choosing instead to move to urban areas and seek employment in shops, factories, coalmines or on the railways, all of which offered better pay and shorter working hours. Of those who returned to their former positions, a large number were made redundant within a few years as a result of landowners scaling down estate operations due to the punitive taxation and death duties imposed by the Lloyd George Liberal government in the aftermath of the war.

World War Two

Landowners once again put their country estates and stately homes at the disposal of the authorities when World War Two was declared. Mansions were taken over by hospitals, schools and businesses, or were used for military operational purposes. Estates provided land for Army camps, airfields, prisoner of war camps, munitions factories, military training grounds and other essential facilities. Gardeners, gamekeepers, farm staff and other skilled workers enlisted in the Army, Royal Navy or Royal Air Force in order to fight for their country, or, later in the war served as 'Bevin Boys' and worked in coal mines. It goes without saying, of course, that far fewer men were employed on estates at this time than at the outbreak of the previous conflict.

Notwithstanding the fact that young, fit and healthy countrymen often made better soldiers and sailors than townies, a large number of estate workers of military age who volunteered to join the armed services were turned down and given reserved occupation status because of their ability to manage land and produce food efficiently. Farm staff and gardeners were generally kept at home along with many gamekeepers and foresters, who combined permitted activities such as vermin control and woodland maintenance with agricultural work. These men not only provided vital food supplies for towns and cities but also made a valuable contribution to the war effort on the Home Front.

The Home Guard

The great majority of estate workers in reserved occupations were recruited into the Home Guard and carried out home defence duties in addition to their normal work, serving alongside men of above military age and those deemed unfit to fight for various reasons. On a number of large sporting properties, including Eaton Hall in Cheshire, Belvoir Castle in Leicestershire and Elveden in Suffolk, estate Home Guard Units were formed, consisting almost entirely of staff members under the command of departmental heads. On Exmoor, the Devon & Somerset Staghounds broke new ground by forming a unique mounted Home Guard unit, the 'Exmoor Mounties', comprising hunt servants, committee members, supporters, gamekeepers, farmers and others, with the Master, Mr S.L. Hancock as C.O. and the huntsman, Ernest Bawden, as section-commander!

Some younger, more active, estate workers were enlisted into top secret elite Home Guard units where they were trained in advanced communications skills and guerrilla warfare in order to defend the country in the event of an enemy invasion. Their brief included sabotaging vehicles, disrupting rail services, attacking important buildings and other essential subversive activities. Sadly, many of these men suffered the humiliation of being labelled as cowards as members of the public could not be told of their important role.

Estate workers, especially those with a larger physique, who did not belong to the Home Guard during World War Two, often served as constables in the Special Constabulary, assisting the regular police with their duties. Other men contributed to the war effort by acting as ARP wardens, as part-time rodent control offices at public establishments based in the countryside, as first aiders or as fire watchers, especially where a country house had been taken over for military use or converted into a hospital or a school.

Arthur Hill, head gamekeeper at Gaddesden Place in Hertfordshire, doubled as a pest control officer at Brocks Fireworks factory in Hemel Hempstead for the duration of World War Two. The factory had temporarily been requisitioned by the government to produce explosives for the armed forces.

Accommodation for senior military officers, land girls and evacuee children

In addition, estate workers provided accommodation for the war effort, billeting senior military officers or housing land girls and Irish farm workers and foresters who had been drafted into the British countryside to replace men who had enlisted in the armed services. Many also took in evacuee children from towns and cities during the war years.

Some estate workers, of course, were killed fighting for their country or died as a result of enemy action. Lance-Bombardier Will' Birdseye, Kennel–huntsman to the Worcester Park and Buckland Beagles, lost his life serving with the 97th Anti-Tank Regiment of the Royal Artillery at Normandy in 1944. Private Reginald Mayes of the Suffolk Regiment, an under-keeper at Thornham Park in Suffolk, died while working on the notorious Burma–Siam railway after being taken prisoner by the Japanese in Singapore. An unnamed gamekeeper on Ruabon Moor in North Wales was killed when his house was bombed by the Luftwaffe after the moor was ignited as a decoy in an attempt to prevent bombing raids on Liverpool.

The cessation of hostilities

Following the cessation of hostilities in the summer of 1945, the estate staff who had remained at home gradually returned to their normal work routine. Sadly, many of those who had joined the armed forces were unable to return to their former jobs or obtain new positions due to agricultural mechanisation and changing game preservation practices, both of which required less manpower.

Some estate workers decided to remain in the Army, often training National Service soldiers who were conscripted during their late teens for a term of around two years. Others joined the Forestry Commission as foresters, pest controllers or warreners, became village tradesmen or left the countryside altogether, lured by the high wages, shorter hours and indoor working environment offered by factories and offices in towns and cities.

Bert Tiller – gamekeeper on the home front

Gamekeepers, in common with other skilled estate employees, made an enormous contribution to the war effort on the Home Front during World War Two, combining their day-to-day work with important defence-related duties. Bert Tiller, head keeper to Lord and Lady Louis Mountbatten (later created Earl and Countess Mountbatten of Burma) on the 6,000 acre Broadlands estate near Romsey in Hampshire, like many of his gamekeeping contemporaries, served in the Home Guard during the war years. At the same time he continued to keep a large country house shoot ticking over to the best of his ability. A veteran of World War One, when he had fought with the Wiltshire Regiment at Hill 60, Vimy Ridge, the Battle of the Somme and in other notable conflicts, he was forty-two years of age when war was declared on 3. September 1939 and had been in charge of the Broadlands game department since 1926.

Above: Private Reginald Mayes, an under-keeper at Thornham Park in Suffolk who enlisted in the Suffolk Regiment shortly after the outbreak of World War Two, was taken prisoner by the Japanese in Singapore and died while working on the notorious Burma–Siam Railway. *Courtesy of M. Brown*

Left: Bert Tiller while serving with the Wiltshire Regiment during World War One c1916. *Courtesy of B. Whittle*

Below: Bert Tiller (on right) on the rearing field at Broadlands prior to being appointed head gamekeeper c1924. *Courtesy of B. Whittle*

The outbreak of war was to have little immediate impact on Bert. Broadlands mansion became an annexe to the Royal South Hants Hospital and the walled park was requisitioned as an Army camp, but otherwise the estate remained much the same. He and his team of four under-keepers continued to run the shoot as normal for the 1939 season. In addition to putting on driven days for Lord Mountbatten when he was home on leave from the Royal Navy, he regularly went out shooting himself accompanied by the estate land agent, Commander North, and a number of local Guns of long standing. The total annual bag taken in 1939, as recorded in his personal game book, amounted to 8,685 head, including 1,135 pheasants, 128 partridges and 7,145 rabbits, along with small quantities of woodcock, snipe, hares and other quarry species.

Nevertheless, Bert built an underground air raid shelter at the bottom of his garden during his spare time, in order to protect himself and his family from the effects of any stray enemy bombs aimed at Southampton Docks, some 6 miles away. He also took on the role of custodian of the Mountbatten family papers for the duration of the war. Packed into a collection of metal trunks, these were entrusted to him by Lady Mountbatten, who instructed him to bury them in his garden at a pre-arranged location. He had been shown the contents before they were sealed in his presence to ensure that he knew that there was no money or jewellery hidden among the papers.

Early in 1940, two of Bert's under-keepers were called up for military service, leaving him with only two men to assist with game preservation on the Broadlands estate. Shortly afterwards he was obliged to give up pheasant rearing after newly enacted legislation made it a criminal offence to rear game birds for sport using grain

and other foodstuffs. Like many other keepers at this time, he culled a large proportion of his pheasant stock for food.

In the summer of 1940, Bert enlisted in the Broadlands estate unit of the newly formed Home Guard and was appointed sergeant. His brief included training new recruits in gunnery and fieldcraft and acting as armourer. He was given permission by his employer, Lord Mountbatten, to arm his men with sporting guns and rifles from the Broadlands gun room as an interim measure until the War Office was able to supply them with Army rifles!

It was not unusual for Bert to work a twelve- or fourteen-hour day gamekeeping before going out on patrol in the countryside at night with his Home Guard colleagues, keeping a lookout for any enemy servicemen who may have parachuted in under the cover of darkness, either as spies or escaping from damaged aircraft, and for any suspicious characters lurking in the vicinity of the Broadlands Army camp. He and his under-keepers also carried out bomb drop patrols on the estate every morning, searching for drop sites of any unexploded bombs, which were mapped and duly reported to the relevant authorities.

Life in the Home Guard was not without incident for Bert, though. In August 1941, he was told to prepare himself for a possible trip to America on secret business, which, according to members of his family, was to involve accompanying Lord Mountbatten and other servicemen on a tour around the USA to persuade the Americans to join the war. Surviving correspondence regarding the matter, while not stating the actual reason for the visit, does confirm that it was ultimately rendered unnecessary and cancelled.

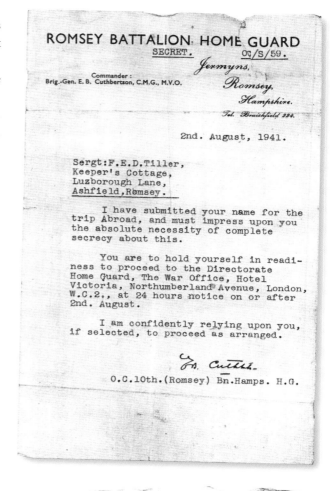

Bert contributed to the war effort in other ways, too, along with his wife, Dorrie. They provided billet accommodation in their house for two Scottish foresters who had been sent by the authorities to manage the woodlands on the Broadland estate, and allowed people from nearby Southampton to sleep in their outbuildings at night to avoid enemy bombing raids. Dorrie also did a little gamekeeping as and when required and assisted on the Broadlands' home farm during busy periods.

Throughout the war years, Bert continued to keep the Broadlands shoot running on a very low-key basis through nest management and vermin control. He and his two remaining under-keepers, Peter Clark and Walter Geary, carried out anti-poaching patrols as often as they could to try to curtail such activities, usually carried out by local people who were after a rabbit or a pheasant for the pot to augment

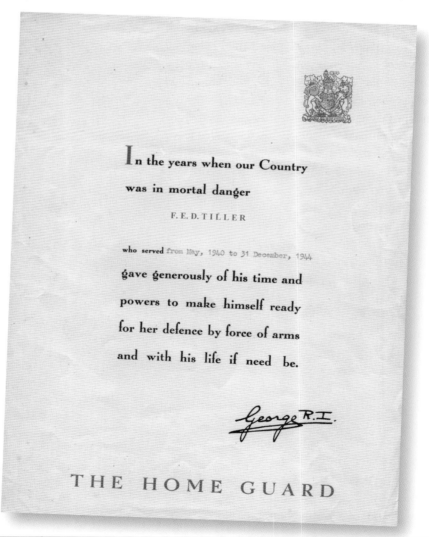

In the years when our Country
was in mortal danger

F. E. D. TILLER

who served from May, 1940 to 31 December, 1944
gave generously of his time and
powers to make himself ready
for her defence by force of arms
and with his life if need be.

George R.I.

THE HOME GUARD

Above and right: Defence Medal and Certificate of thanks awarded to Bert Tiller in recognition of his services in the Home Guard during World War Two.

their meagre meat rations or soldiers based on the estate who fancied game for their supper in preference to standard Army fare. Bert and his men regularly killed large numbers of rabbits, supplying them to butchers and game dealers in Southampton and elsewhere to help out with wartime food shortages, and held a rabbit sale on the estate every Friday for the benefit of members of the Royal South Hants Hospital staff employed in the mansion.

From time to time Bert arranged walked-up and small-scale driven shoots for Army officers based on the estate and friends and relatives of the Mountbatten family who were on leave from the services. It was not unusual for between twenty-five and seventy-five pheasants to be shot on a good day, along with a few partridges and hares. Pheasants were either given away locally, sold to the Polygon Hotel in Southampton or sent to a cold store on Southampton Docks rented by the Broadlands estate, where they were kept until required for family consumption.

For nearly six long years, Bert Tiller, did his bit for the war effort on the Home Front. Like many other gamekeepers who joined the Home Guard, he was presented with a certificate of thanks signed by King George VI and awarded the Defence Medal for his services. He went on to rebuild the Broadlands shoot to its former glory in the aftermath of the war, but that is another story!

ESTIMATES
on *Application* for
Conservatories
Ranges
Orchid Houses
Improved
Frames
Boilers
Heating
Apparatus
etc.

LARGE STOCK OF
SEASONED
TEAK.

ESTABLISHED 1841.

Conservatories Designed to Harmonize with Dwelling Houses

BEESTON, NOTTS.

Supplied also by the "C.G.A." Letchworth, Herts ; 127 St. Vincent Street, Glasgow ;
and 41 Grafton Street, Dublin.

Advertisement for
a country house
conservatory, 1916.

BIBLIOGRAPHY,
FURTHER READING,
REFERENCES AND SOURCES

Adams, Samuel and Sarah: *The Complete Servant*; 1825.

'Amateur Sportsman': *Sporting Anecdotes*; J. Cundee & J. Harris, 1807.

Baily's Hunting Directory 1908–1909: Vinton & Co. Ltd, 1908.

Baily's Hunting Directory 1916–1917; Vinton & Co. Ltd, 1916.

Battrick, Jack: *Brownsea Islander*; Poole Historical Trust, 1978.

Bearstall, T.W: *A North Country Estate*; Phillimore & Co. Ltd, 1975.

Bollans, C. Alan: *Thoresby Park*; published privately, 2000.

Braithwaite, Geoffrey: *Fine Feathers and Fish*: published privately, 1971.

Brooks, Alan: Woodlands – *A Practical Handbook*; B.T.C.V., 1980.

Brown, Robert E.: *The Book of the Landed Estate*; William Blackwood and Sons, 1869.

Caird, James, *English Agriculture in* 1850–51; 1852.

Denys, Bt., Sir Francis: *Sporting Journal*; unpublished manuscript.

Devonshire, 11th Duchess of: *The House: A Portrait of Chatsworth*; Macmillan London Ltd., 1982.

Ellis, Maudie A: *The Squire of Bentley (Mrs Cheape)*; William Blackwood & Sons Ltd, 1926.

Fairclough, John and Hardy, Mike: *Thornham and the Waveney Valley – An Historic Landscape Explored*; Heritage Marketing & Publications Ltd, 2004.

Fielding, Daphne: *Mercury Presides*; Eyre & Spottiswode, 1954.

Field, The: various articles, 1858 and 1868.

Forbes, A.C: *English Estate Forestry*; Edward Arnold, 1906.

Gamekeeper, The: 1897–1940.

Hawkins, Desmond: *Cranborne Chase*; Victor Gollancz Ltd, 1980.

Heber-Percy, Cyril: *Us Four*; Faber & Faber, 1963.

Hennell, Thomas: *Change In The Farm*; Cambridge University Press, 1936.

Jones, David S.D: *Gamekeepers, Gypsies and Poachers – The Family Tree of Elizabeth Grass of Brandon*: published privately, 1994 (second edition 2014).

Jones, David S.D.: *Gamekeeping: An Illustrated History*; Quiller, 2014.

Jones, David S.D.: *Harry Grass – King of the Gamekeepers*; published privately, 2011.

Jones, David S.D.: *The Cambrook House Story: The History of a Somerset Workhouse*; published privately, 1996.

Jones, David S.D: *The David S.D. Jones Gamekeeping and Countryside Archive and Photographic Collection*.

Kitchen, Fred: *Brother to the Ox*; J.M. Dent & Sons Ltd, 1939.

Knight, Frank & Rutley: *Lilleshall Estate Sale Catalogue* 1917.

Londonderry, Marchioness of: *Henry Chaplin – A Memoir*; Macmillan & Co., 1926.

Montagu of Beaulieu, Lord and Macnaghten, Patrick: *Home James – The Chauffeur in the Golden Age of Motoring*; Weidenfeld and Nicolson, 1982.

Portland, 6th Duke of: *Men, Women and Things*; Faber & Faber, 1938.

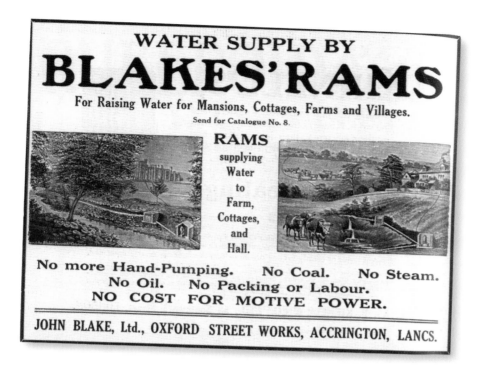

Advertisement for Blake's Rams, a system commonly use to provide a water supply for country houses, farms and estate village prior to the introduction of mains water. Dated 1916.

Ridley, George: *Bend'or, Duke of Westminster*; Robin Clark Ltd, 1985.

Smart, Ron and Wellings, Richard: *Worcestershire Woodin' – Hazel Woods in a Nutshell*; Small Woods Association, 2009.

Spring, David: *The English Landed Estate in the Nineteenth Century: Its Administration*; The Johns Hopkins Press, USA, 1963.

Sutherland, 5th Duke of: *Looking Back*; Odhams Press Ltd., 1957.

Taylor, David J: *I Remember Normanby*; Scunthorpe Museums and the Hutton Press Ltd., 1994.

Thornton, Henry G: *Hunting Journal*; unpublished manuscript.

Turner, Tom: *Memoirs of a Gamekeeper; (Elveden, 1868–1953)*; Geoffrey Bles, 1954.

Watson, Alfred E.T: *English Sport*; Macmillan & Co., 1903.

Wood, Donald: *Bolton Abbey – The Time of my Life*; published privately, 1996.